REPORTING
THE WAR
IN UKRAINE

A First Draft of History

EDITED BY
JOHN MAIR
(with Andrew Beck)

Published 2022 by Abramis academic publishing

www.abramis.co.uk

ISBN 978 1 84549 802 3

© John Mair 2022

Typeset in Garamond

Abramis is an imprint of arima publishing.

arima publishing
ASK House, Northgate Avenue
Bury St Edmunds, Suffolk IP32 6BB
t: (+44) 01284 717884

www.arimapublishing.com

Contents

Acknowledgements

Curated books are sums of their parts. Writers have to be commissioned, cajoled and corrected (usually minimally) before publication. These books have breakneck schedules. I am writing this just 100 days after Putin's invasion of Ukraine. The writing has been quick and very often simply superb. I thank all the contributors for their work and their patience in the face of my email harassment. They are the stars of the war reporting and of this volume.

Andrew Beck was my proof-reader and conscience. I thank him.

I am also as ever grateful to Richard and Pete Franklin at Abramis for their publishing skills, to Dean Stockton for an (as ever) brilliant cover and to my ever patient wife Susan Ann who confined me to the dining table during lockdown. Still there and still creating volume after volume.

John Mair, Oxford, 3 June 2022

The Editor

John Mair is the most prolific editor/author on matters journalistic in Britain. This is his 47th 'hackademic' book mixing hacks and academics in short order. He helped to invent the genre. Subjects have ranged from the Leveson Report to the future of the BBC to the pandemic to more recently the Oxford of Inspector Morse and the huge oil boom in his native land-Guyana - 'Oil Dorado'. John was a BBC (and other broadcasters) producer and a teacher of journalism in previous lives. He lives in Oxford.

The world is now a very dangerous place. Russia after Putin's army is defeated

John Simpson is a world figure in broadcasting. He's been in the BBC for 55 years. Covered too many wars to list. Today he is their World Affairs Editor. Here in an edited extract from a recent Oxford lecture he muses on life post Putin

The world is a very, very dangerous place. If Vladimir Putin starts to look as though he's been badly defeated in Ukraine and if he starts to think that people in Russia will interpret what's happened to him as being a defeat then who knows what might happen.

Russian military orthodoxy says, unlike Western military orthodoxy, that actually you can, if you get into a hole, use tactical nuclear weapons. That's they say, small yield and small direct. Nuclear bombs, which might affect a city, might destroy a city, but wouldn't necessarily have effects too far beyond that one city.

This is of course something that hasn't happened in the world since 1945. And nobody knows at the moment what Nato's response would be including Nato. There are a lot of people inside Nato with different views of what should be done under that. But there's no clear Nato policy. That will have to be made on the hoof. If and when if, it happens and we've got to pray that it (tactical nuclear attack) won't happen.

Why should there have been this shift in Putin's Russia?

I think it started about 2012. I interviewed him, I met him various times. He was still a fairly open-minded person, actually personally, quite pleasant and what's happened to him now. Something has definitely happened, whether it's illness, whether it's the situation in Russia, which forces him to behave as he has done. We can't know that really from the outside, we'll find out one day, we don't at the moment, but that is what happened.

The Great Russian Army?

In many ways, it's the most aggressive army so of course they're going to win. Well, we saw what happened to that. They couldn't even capture Kvij even though it was only a matter of forty miles from the border, that wasn't in their grasp. And they've had to do this extraordinary thing - retreat - which military historians will be looking at for decades, if not longer, to come.

They have been forced to move the entire thrust of their attack from the capital Kvij in the centre of Ukraine, to the east where they're more capable of being successful. Even now they're not that successful. So that's one reason really, for optimism; in many ways the second biggest and supposedly most aggressive army in the world actually turned out to be pretty feeble.

Life after Ukraine for Putin

Somebody asked me about what would happen in Russia. And I said, and I feel this very strongly that at some stage it's all going to come back and hit Putin. He's not, I think, going to just live his life out like Stalin did for instance, and die in his bed.

I'm pretty confident of that. Who knows you can't be certain, but it's a different world from Stalin's world. And I, I don't think Putin is going to last the course. What will happen then? Supposing that somebody comes to Putin, either a military guy or another politician and says, 'Look, I'm sorry, but it's over. You can go and sit in your dacha, or many dachas and just be quiet and we're taking over the work of the government.' I think that must be quite a possibility. I know, not immediately, but in a matter of years, no doubt.

What does a government that's taken over under difficult circumstances with the enmity of the West, still reverberating around the economy and, and in diplomatic terms, what do you do?

War Crimes?

And at that stage, if that happens in Russia at that stage, Vladimir Putin will appear at the Hague or perhaps he won't make it all the way. Who knows? There's never been a set of war crimes and human rights violations, which has been so thoroughly, so well, documented as to what's been happening.

There was you'll perhaps remember appalling events in Bucha, just outside of Kvij. Unthinkable things, which it's best not even to think about. We know the names of every single, one of the Russian soldiers who was involved in that. And we have their photographs so we know what villages they come from back home.

Those men are not going to live out their lives in peace and comfort. You can be absolutely certain about that. At some stage, those men will be on trial and will hopefully spend the rest of their lives in jail.

Is Putin well?

Well, I look at him and there he is puffy. I saw some video of him the other day. I can't remember who it was, came to visit him. And he was standing there for quite a long time. And he suddenly weirdly raised his hand and started kind of shaking it before you reached over and shook the hand of whoever the visitor was. And when he walked, he walked very awkwardly. But you know, he is 69. I don't know how good a life he leads in terms of exercise and food and so on. And maybe the puffiness. He could say the same about me. What do you think Parkinson's is? Or? I've no idea, but I mean it wouldn't be altogether unlikely.

Why did he invade Ukraine?

I think the key thing is that this invasion was hatched during his two years of Covid. He seemed to be terrified of getting it. He only saw very, very few people and those very few people that he saw and just told him what he wanted to hear. And, in particular, they told him that the people of Ukraine would welcome and greet the Russian soldiers as liberators, is exactly what the Russians said to themselves and to their soldiers in Hungary in 1956. It's exactly what they said to their soldiers in 1968 in Czechoslovakia when they invaded that. And for all I know they probably said the same thing when they invaded Afghanistan in 1979. That sense that you will be greeted and welcome.

People support Putin for all sorts of different reasons. It's the part of the population that watches television believes basically what it's told. And that part is mostly, I'm afraid, older people over the age of 50, 55, something like that.

They're told these very graphic things and they're given a tremendous assurance night after night after night, about how our boys are doing so well, how that it's only just the neo-Nazis in Ukraine that are holding out against them and so on. They, they believe it because there's not much else now. There was a wonderful television station, which had enormous courage and was still until about two months ago putting out a pretty honest version of what was really going on in their world. But that's all gone now and all you see is state TV. Russian television is a version really of *Fox TV* only to the ultimate, full of loud, angry blowhards, some of whom as you saw the other day, talk openly about, destroying the British Isles with nuclear weapons.

I think if Russia comes out of this badly as I suspect it will, or at least if not badly, then it will seem not to have been successful. Their enormous military actually couldn't get it together. Then I think that will have a major influence on a lot of countries.

It's always going to be a battle. It always has been a battle, but we shouldn't forget that the liberal democracies did actually defeat, Marxism-Leninism in Russia right throughout Eastern Europe.

Note on lecture

This is an edited version of the My Jericho lecture delivered by John Simpson in St Barnabas Church Jericho on 8 May 2022.

About the contributor

John Simpson CBE is the World Affairs editor of the BBC. He has worked for the Corporation for 55 years and reported from 120 countries. In his time he has been the Political Editor and the presenter of the main evening news inter alia.

Introduction

John Mair

'The inescapable hurry of the press inevitably means a certain degree of superficiality. It is neither within our power nor our province to be ultimately profound. We write 365 days a year the first rough draft of history, and that is a very great task.'

Philip Graham, Publisher Washington Post, 1953

3 June 2022

One hundred days after the Russian invasion of Ukraine. The battle goes back and forth on the Donbas front. Who knows when and where this war will end? Who will 'win' and who will 'lose'. This book attempts a first rough draft of history, mainly through the eyes of journalistic observers to start to provide some answers. The names who have written dispatches for it are well known in many households. None have been paid.

The great John Simpson of the BBC provides an overview to kick it all off.

In the first, discrete, section 'FROM THE FRONTLINE' reporters report from the Ukrainian frontline. Stuart Ramsay of *Sky News* relives his close brush with death with Russians out to kill him and his team. His boss John Ryley shares his angst of the time and Mark Grant, the *Sky News* security head, reveals some of the measures they take to keep correspondents like Stuart alive. Alex Thompson of *Channel Four News* too had a close call. He was one car away from being blown apart. He relives that. Paul Kenyon of the *BBC's Panorama* is already a Ukraine war old hand. He has made three half-hour programmes in the 100 days. Kenyon tells the stories of those brutalised by the Russian 31st Brigade in their failed assault on Kvij before they moved East. Orla Guerin of the BBC and Rohit Kachroo of *ITV News* are very seasoned war hands. 'Firemen' in the jargon of journalism - they run towards conflicts rather than away. They both tell harrowing stories of real people caught up in geopolitics and the often tragic consequences. Orla's story of the dead child's memento given to her is especially chilling.

Two non-aligned journalists, Dan Morgan and Azaz Safarov, bring different perspectives. Morgan hitch-hiked his way to perform his photography craft on the front line. Safarov is the fixers fixer but he also has a double life as the organiser of an NGO dedicated to helping children traumatised by war.

Ukraine 2022 has been the ultimate television war. Gruesome pictures and reports night after night and day after day on the network news. The broadcast stars have been queueing up to get to the Kyiv and beyond. The less brave have made it just to Lviv in the west or the Polish border. Clive Myrie is, so far, one of the standout stars.

Ukraine and President Zelenskyy have exploited the medium as the message/ massage to the fullest. He has not turned down a remote gig to parliaments and gatherings worldwide. Nightly too he has kept up the spirits of his countrymen and women using Zoom. The Ukrainians have also refined their regime of censorship so subtly as to be almost invisible - apart from to the journalists who cross their red lines. Was the truth embedded with the reporters assigned to Ukrainian army units? That story remains to be told.

Jim White, a great writer on sport for the *Daily Telegraph*, turns his pen to the war media. He points out that the Ukrainians need Western TV there to keep the message in the public's eyes and the weapons flowing to them. No publicity, no horror stories, no sophisticated weapons supplied. Andrew Beck provides a very interesting academic view of British TV and newspaper coverage to date using the words of the reporters.

Print journalism has been left playing catch up on this war. Put simply, the war is on screens nightly in glorious colour. News is stale the next morning so the national papers are left searching for obtuse angles. Richard Pendelbury of the *Daily Mail* provides two fascinating off-diary encounters away from the 'bang bang' while Kim Sengupta of the *Independent* traces one man through at least three wars in the Ukraine. The perceptive media commentator Liz Gerard provides some background on the atrophy of foreign desks and foreign correspondents in Fleet Street as the revenue streams have dried up

In the second distinct section 'A LITTLE EUROPEAN WAR?' we move beyond the 'bang bang' to cyberspace. This is no conventional war. It has been labelled the *Tik-Tok* war for the emergence of social media as a tool of war. Bellingcat has become a star of this show. They simply use open source intelligence geolocation, meta data, etc. - to expose Russian propaganda or simply lies. Nick Waters explains how it is done. Dr Dominic Selwood examines the rise of a new military secret weapon, the drone, and the people behind it. Dr Alex Connock writes on new trends in an intelligent way and calls it the AI (Artificial Intelligence) War and explains why. Dr Paul Lashmar, an academic and journalist who has specialised in intelligence matters, welcomes the new openness of Western intelligence agencies. That has paid dividends. Finally, in this section former Fleet Street Editor Paul Connew asks if the Ukraine fairy story will have a happy ending.

In the last section 'A LITTLE EUROPEAN WAR BECOMES A GLOBAL CONFLICT' a variety of authors take non UK perspectives. Jon Williams looks at the extraordinary kindness of Irish people to refugees with institutional memories of the great Irish potato famine of 1845-49 and the migration tsunami that generated world-wide. Carolyn Jackson-Brown reads the runes and framing of the media with some undergraduate and postgraduate students in Leeds. They firmly are the *Tik-Tok* generation. If it is not on that platform then it cannot be true. Pulitzer Prize winner David Cay Johnson detects an abrupt change in reporting this war by US journalists. They were much more forewarned about this war, dealt in by open US intelligence, and much more likely to take the side of the plucky Ukrainians.

China is supposedly neutral in this conflict. We have two contrasting angles on that. Dr Yan Wu finds Chinese journalists remiss in their journalism thanks to Central Party control, whilst Marcus Ryder - who has worked in the Chinese media - offers a plague on both Western and Chinese media houses.

The Russian side has been absent from any world coverage. Partly through design by not allowing access to their military, partly through shutting down intendent media in the country but mainly by feeding their population propaganda through a pliant state media. Professor Ivor Gaber looks to social psychology to try to explain why the population is so accepting of half-truths, whilst Robin Aitken of the *Daily Telegraph* takes a counter-intuitive position, saying too much of our coverage is based on Russophobia.

Deborah Haynes Security and Defence Editor of *Sky News* adds some geo-political perspective in her end note about the Russians and why they invaded Ukraine.

All in all, a rough but a comprehensive first draft of history of the first 100 days of the 2022 Ukraine war.

Where the war and history ends for Ukraine is still a very open question.

ON THE FRONTLINE

***

'Don't let the bastards get away with it!' Near death on the frontline

At the start of the Russian invasion of Ukraine in February 2022 , *Sky News'* chief correspondent Stuart Ramsay and his team, after reporting for two months in the country's east, found themselves in Kyiv, awaiting an expected lightning attack on the capital. They endured days of air raid sirens, mass evacuations, and enforced curfews, the team headed out to a previously unheard-of town to the northwest of Kyiv. They were heading for Bucha; they didn't make it. On their return journey they came under fire

'Where are you going?'

The words cut through the momentary silence of the rushes of our last trip.

There is no answer on the tape.

I only know those words were said because three of us are sitting and watching in silence the images and sounds that will stay with us for the rest of our lives, played out on a tiny viewing screen in a Ukrainian hotel room.

'I didn't know what you were doing,' says Richie Mockler, who filmed the pictures we are playing and rewinding as we prepare to begin the editing process, 'it was mental'.

My producer Dominique Van Heerden looks over as I start pacing around the room, it's a habit.

'Yeah, mental,' she says, and goes back to the images.

The low glow of light from the edit computer and the reflection of the images in their eyes accompanied by the ominous sounds of war is a scene I have experienced countless times over the past few decades in countries around the world.

In recent years mainly with these two friends.

'Where are you going, what are you doing?'

Aren't those two of the biggest questions we all face in some shape or form throughout life? I thought to myself.

Certainly, they are fundamental questions that all journalists, particularly those working in the rarefied atmosphere of war, must answer; another, much asked, is: 'Why?'

The much quoted and to be honest, remarkably accurate, motivation for conflict reporting is to bear witness.

It has to be the fundamental reason. If we don't go the bastards get away with it, as the old adage goes.

Equally importantly is that if we don't go, we don't know what is happening to the civilians; particularly the young, the old, the poor and weak.

If you believe in these basic principles of reporting, you may not be able to answer the 'where are you going?' but you will always know why, whatever the context.

The invasion

It is the morning of day five of the Russian invasion, Monday 28 February 2022.

Two of the previous four days we have been stuck in our Kyiv hotel observing a strict curfew imposed by Ukrainian security forces trying to track down so called Russian 'saboteurs' who they claimed were attacking civilians and carrying out acts of terror.

Up early, Dominique, called a meeting of the team.

We met in the hotel's deserted café. Just us and the staff were left now.

Producers Martin Vowles and Andrii Lytvynenko nodded agreement along with Richie and I as Dominique pointed out two fundamentals: we could hear the sounds of war but couldn't see anything in the city, and we knew civilians were being killed, even targeted, and needed to tell that story.

Knowing you need to go see is all well and good, actually doing it in a newly developing conflict where the only thing you can say for certain is that you have absolutely no idea what is going on, raises a fair amount of concern about the danger.

We elected to travel to a town where we had contacts who said some initial fighting had calmed down, but that there were casualties and the remnants of a Russian armoured convoy that had been destroyed.

We had never heard of the place, but it wasn't far.

We headed for Bucha.

Dozens of checkpoints and many hours of travelling later we were nearing the town.

In the sky Russian helicopter gunships criss-crossed the battlefield a few kilometres ahead of us.

Ukrainian soldiers said the fighting had intensified and had no idea where the front line was any more which made going forward treacherous at best, suicidal more likely.

It was late afternoon; our story plan had been thwarted by the fighting, so we decided to call it a day.

Under fire

Our routes in were now part of the battle space so we had to find another way out.

A police checkpoint pointed us towards Kyiv.

We headed off. It was deadly quiet. We approached an intersection, there was rubble on the road, but that is normal. There were no soldiers, it seemed deserted.

Then an explosion and I saw something hit the car and a tyre burst, we rolled to a stop.

Silence.

One of us swore as the first round cracked the windscreen.

Richie, in the front passenger seat, dropped to the floor.

Dominique in the back did the same, and I lay on my side across the backseat.

Martin, who was driving, and Andrii, also in the back, made a run for it.

Then we were under full attack from the front and the left side.

Bullets cascaded through the vehicle, tracers flashed, sparks, glass flying around us, the constant whizz of rounds and the car slowly disintegrated.

We didn't know it, but we were being ambushed by an alleged Russian reconnaissance squad, at the time we thought it was a mistake by a Ukrainian checkpoint.

In a lull in the shooting, we started screaming we were journalists.

If anything, the shooting intensified.

Bullets filled the car

It was professional, the rounds kept smashing into the car. They wanted to kill us.

We knew we had to get out, but the fire was intense.

Dominique slipped through the open car door and to the ground, crawling beneath a motorway barrier and rolling down a 40-foot embankment to the bottom.

Richie was shouting to me. I can't remember what he was saying but I think he said he was hit. He took two rounds to his body armour.

Bullets continued to fill the car and I remember thinking 'I'm going to die; I wonder if it will hurt'.

Then I was hit. The bullet entered the top part of my left leg and exited through my lower back.

It felt like a hammer blow with sparklers fizzing through my side.

It was strange but I felt calm.

I put my helmet on and was about to attempt my escape but stopped and reached back into a shelf in the door and picked up my phones.

Ignoring the shooting I stepped out of the car and stood up, then jogged, as best I could, to the edge of the embankment. I took two steps then fell to the bottom, landing on my head.

Richie was still inside. The rounds kept ploughing into the car, but he was being protected by the engine block.

He called out and we shouted for him to come - then silence.

It seemed like an eternity before he emerged over the motorway barrier and jumped down towards us followed by a hail of gunfire.

At the bottom we regrouped. The five of us were alive. We couldn't believe it.

In shock but somewhat elated we made our way along a slip road and dived inside the gate of a warehouse unit where three caretakers beckoned for us to come inside.

Outside the shooting continued.

We were convinced our assailants would come for us and that at any moment the garage doors would explode inwards, and gunmen would come to kill us.

Dominique took my phone and with our local staff planned our escape. It would take many hours of negotiation and calls to every contact our producers had ever had.

In the darkness and cold of the warehouse we found a small room where we planned to huddle together to keep warm.

As my eyes closed the sounds of shouting and heavy boots came up the stairwell.

Then these beautiful words: 'Ukrainian police, come quickly!'

There was still a long way to go. But we had been rescued.

Targeted attacks on civilians

The real point of this story is that it illustrates what we have come to know about the Russian operation in Ukraine and why eyewitness journalism is so vitally important.

This was not an attack on journalists; this was an attack on civilians.

We were driving in a family saloon car. It wasn't marked "PRESS" or "TV" on the advice of the Ukrainian authorities, who said that Russian agents were driving around in cars marked as "PRESS", which the Ukrainian forces were looking out for.

In the days and weeks that passed more and more attacks on innocent civilians took place, many of whom were fleeing, and the true number of people killed remains unknown.

What we believe is that, unwittingly, we had driven into the very early stages of the Russian military's plan to enter Kyiv from the west.

We were travelling on the M06 and E40 motorways. CCTV footage and a host of news organisations have identified the killing of civilians in their cars on this same road.

There appears to have been a concerted effort, a specific tactic, by the Russians to bring fear, violence and death as a tool of its war, as opposed to a consequence of it.

We hadn't heard of Bucha as we attempted to get there. But we all do now.

A satellite town to Kyiv previously of no import has become the centre of a war crimes investigation that will doubtless expand as evidence of further Russian atrocities is collected from the areas where they took control, and the people made it clear they were not welcome.

We were lucky of course, and we have training and body armour. Countless civilians neither had our luck or our equipment.

Richie, Dominique and I sat in silence, preparing to edit our story.

'Where are you going?' played again.

I couldn't have answered Richie, even if I had heard him, as I stepped out of the car. But I had to keep going, I had to get out. We all knew that.

None of the journalists covering this war know exactly where we are going at any given time.

But we all know why: we are bearing witness so the bastards don't get away with it.

It's simple really.

Home

'Are you queasy?' my surgeon asked me as I lay on my side in an operating theatre in Oxford.

'That is what I have taken out of you,' he said, reaching around my body so I could see a bowl of flesh: my flesh, my bullet wound, my body.

I didn't know what to say really.

I was cleaned up and stitched up. I was good to go.

In the car home I giggled continuously. I was hysterical. I hadn't expected anything so traumatic as that operation to remove the core of my bullet wound. Think of an apple being de-cored. That is what happened to me.

All of us returned home after the attack.

It took about five days to get back to Britain.

They were traumatic days. We left Kyiv and drove 18 hours to Lviv, where we edited for a day, and I saw a surgeon who recommended I get back to the UK.

At the airport we said our emotional goodbyes.

A week later, just before being de-cored, the surgeon told me I was one of the luckiest people he had ever met.

Dominique, Richie, Martin, and Andrii also all went home to their families.

We have all suffered from the stress of this incident. It comes in waves and affects everyone differently. But everyone feels good now.

Aftershock, May 2022

We are going back to Ukraine.

Dominique sent me a message telling me to sort my kit and make sure everything was okay, that nothing was permanently damaged.

I hadn't emptied my armour bag since we returned.

I pulled out my flak jacket and noticed a bullet hole and a tear on the back. Then another, and another, and another, and another, and another.

A suspicious marking on my helmet, a strange graze on the inside of my flak jacket ... It is my birthday.

I sat down and I cried.

All this time I thought I was lucky to be wounded by a single bullet.

I hadn't been so lucky. I had been hammered, but I was saved by my armour.

I cried because, although I have said it dozens of times in conversations and interviews, we survived because of our training and our gear and of course with a load of luck.

So many families, mums and dads with their kids and grandparents, have not.

I wrote to Dominique: 'Oh Fuck!' She replied:

'You need new armour.'

Video of the attack on Stuart and his team

https://news.sky.com/story/sky-news-teams-harrowing-account-of-their-violent-ambush-in-ukraine-this-week-12557585**.

About the contributor

Stuart Ramsay is chief correspondent at Sky News, reporting on major global news stories and world events - including over 20 separate wars during his 30-year career.

He has been posted to bureaux in Russia, the United States, South Africa, India and Dubai, and is Sky's longest-serving foreign correspondent.

In March 2020, Stuart was the first to expose the full-scale of the COVID-19 pandemic with his searing, Emmy award-winning reportage from inside hospitals in northern Italy. Stuart has been covering the war in Ukraine since 2014.

Managing risk on a changing frontline

They are usually in the shadows - the security advisors who are the sine qua non today for frontline war reporters. They keep them safe and alive. Here, in an exclusive for this book, Dr Mark Grant, who heads up *Sky News* security, takes us behind the veil in the Ukraine

Getting journalists to the frontline while also trying to keep them safe is the job of professional security advisors who are rarely mentioned or even seen. But their job is considered by their companies as vitally important. The war in Ukraine has become one of the deadliest conflicts for journalists to report: two big countries in conflict is unusual in the modern era. So many of the lessons that have been learnt about safety in the past are having to be rewritten virtually hour by hour.

I was sitting in the Intercontinental Hotel in Kyiv on 28 February 2022 when my phone started ringing. The name 'Stuart Ramsay' appeared on my screen. It was just after 4pm. I had a sinking feeling that something was wrong because the team had checked in only minutes earlier saying they were 'all good' and heading back to the city centre.

The person on the other end of the phone was Dominique Van Heerden, the team's producer, and with the calmest of voices, she said 'Mark, we've been ambushed…'

You know the rest of the story.

This war is bloody dangerous. Prepare

This, along with another two incidents with other teams all within the first five days of the war in Ukraine, in my mind, cemented this as the most dangerous, fast-paced, and challenging conflict I have ever covered.

Just two weeks earlier I'd returned to the UK from a four week trip to Afghanistan. It was a quick turnaround for me because we were trying to get multiple *Sky News* teams into Ukraine to bolster our coverage, and do it safely.

Within 12 hours of arriving back from Kabul I was on the phone with our Head of International News working out how we'd deploy.

24 hours later I was checking in for an early morning Whizz Air flight from Gatwick Airport, with more than 250kg of ballistic vests, helmets, medical kits and other safety equipment.

As you might imagine this made for an interesting sight as I struggled with three luggage trolleys. All the porters were busy tending to the world's media, all with the same idea, all trying to board the same flight, all with their own trolleys full of gear.

It was in that moment I realised that Ukraine would likely be the largest concentrated deployment of news crews for years. Not since Iraq and Syria in 2018 had I witnessed such a large grouping of journalists in one location, and it felt more like a reunion than a deployment.

Fluid frontlines

Although our planning for the Ukraine conflict had started months before, and although *Sky News* already has robust risk management processes in place, some of the most competent journalists within the industry, and a well-resourced security and safety set up, the early days of the conflict were changing every day, sometimes every hour.

There were so many variables to manage, almost all plans and assessments we conducted had to be reassessed daily. Without this set-up, support and understanding of risk, we would have likely had a very different outcome to the one we had for Stuart Ramsay's team.

Of course, this is not specific to *Sky News* , and there are several anecdotal stories from others in similar security roles supporting news crews, especially those who had multiple teams, deployed across multiple locations in Ukraine.

In the days immediately after the start of the war, there were several critical changes, almost daily, often causing frustrations and creating ambiguity on the most effective way to operate. From the changing of laws in country for journalists, the rules around what could be gathered, and what could not be aired. The implementation of curfews on a city level, ongoing changes with press accreditation and overall nervousness by Ukrainians were just some of the issues that needed constant navigating in the early days.

Locals and journos flee West to Lviv

The day the war started, many fixers and translators, local producers and drivers, working with Western journalists decided to head west towards Lviv. Some were on 'wanted' lists distributed online by the Russian authorities, others wanted to be with and protect their families, something most people would, understandably, do.

Although morally it was the right thing for them to do, it did leave a huge operational gap in resources, as we scrambled to confirm which of our local support staff would stay, who would go, and who would allow us to continue to use their vehicles.

I've covered many conflicts, but this was a first. I have never been in a position where local staff were not in a position to support our teams.

Some in Ukraine put family before money, and who can blame them.

Arming the population

Another element that created an unexpected risk was the issuing of over 20,000 weapons by the Ukrainian government to a civilian population. They called it National Defence.

These weapons were frequently issued to people with no experience, in remote areas, and some could not tell the difference between a van marked 'PRESS', with all occupants with official accreditation, and that of Russian Forces vehicle with the letter 'V'.

As much as the formation of the National Defence helped Ukrainians arm themselves against impending danger, it also created a tense atmosphere across the country. This resulted in many of our teams moving across Ukraine being harassed, and poorly treated, with one team being pulled from their vehicle at gunpoint and badly beaten.

The power that being armed brings, coupled with the fear and tensions of impending war, meant the presence of the National Defence increased the risk for our journalists, which in many ways is counter-productive because it reduced the coverage of the conflict.

The war in Ukraine is a conventional, and a relatively symmetric war with a huge amount of ordinance available to both sides, however unlike Afghanistan, Iraq or even Syria, the Russian Forces could easily hit locations our news teams extensively operate, including in the capital Kyiv, and they carried out these kinds of attacks regularly.

Indirect fire

The other big risk in this conflict is indirect fire. This is a risk that exists in any conflict, but in Ukraine this risk somehow feels closer. Indirect fire is harder to avoid tactically, with many more 'near misses', reported due to shrapnel fragmentation.

The concept risk versus reward sounds a little clichéd, but it is an important discussion. Having frank, open and often difficult conversations early on with our journalists was the only way we could ensure we could allow teams to operate and gather freely, while also ensuring there was a commensurate level of risk mitigation applied across our coverage.

We are hardly alone in this.

All news organisations face the challenge of balancing the varying experience and expectation levels of our journalists, with the desire to report the story in the most impactful way possible.

Body armour saves lives

Of course, the personal protective equipment they were wearing literally saved their lives.

So back to the phone call on 28 February.

Some would say that Stuart Ramsay and his team were lucky to be alive after their ambush, and while I would not disagree with that, I do believe that several factors played an active part in the somewhat positive outcomes, as much and if not more, than luck on that day.

The team's competence and experience - like knowing how to take effective cover - and their ability to effectively communicate in a crisis, were defining factors and played an active role in their own survival.

I'm aware that often there is a reluctance among journalists to wear and lug around heavy body armour, but in this case, their body armour was the difference between being alive and being dead.

It also gave them confidence to operate effectively knowing they were protected as much as possible.

'This stuff is amazing,' the fixer working with Ramsay's team was studying and commenting on the ballistic vest he had been wearing when they were ambushed. He couldn't believe we had given him personal protective equipment.

In the weeks before he had worked with a news organisation who didn't give him any.

I find this appalling.

Anyone asked to take the same risks we journalists do should be given the same level of protection, no excuses.

The future is brutal

This war in Ukraine is far from over. And the likelihood is there will be even more journalists injured and killed in the weeks and months ahead.

Although this is the brutal reality of covering war and bearing witness to the atrocities carried out, there are ways we can significantly reduce risks to news teams.

What security managers can and should do is provide handrails, not fences.

We can help teams improve on their medical and security competence through education and conversation, we can also help them dynamically assess their assignments, knowing they want to go towards risk … not away from it.

We all know journalists want to do their job. They wouldn't have it any other way.

We may as well try help them to do it safely.

About the contributor

Dr Mark Grant is the High Risk, Safety and Security Lead at *Sky News*. Mark has operated extensively in high-risk environments around the world and has previously supported and managed security for the BBC and CNN. He holds a master's degree and a professional doctorate in Security Risk Management, with specific focus on Journalism Security. Mark is a Co-Founder, and Non-Executive of MiRiskMedia, an App based solution to providing news organisations and freelancers with direct access to vetted, qualified and experienced Safety and Security Advisors.

The Bucha attack on *Sky News*. A test of leadership

'I felt sick,' said the Head of *Sky News*, John Ryley, when he first watched the video of the attack. Discussions - sometimes punchy - took place about what *Sky News* digital and TV audiences should see. He believes it is right to ask correspondents to risk their lives to bear witness provided they have the right training and experience. The attack on Sky's Stuart Ramsay team tested *Sky News* and its leadership, writes John Ryley

Eye-witness journalism

Writing as an old fart of news, I thought I had seen and heard most things, handled most editorial and ethical issues in my 38 years in journalism: as a producer seeing the melted bodies of 12 school children and their teacher who died when their minibus crashed on the M40 in 1993; as an output editor deciding in the moment to broadcast video of people jumping to their deaths from the North Tower of New York's World Trade Center in 2001; and as a boss listening to the sound recording of our camera operator, the dear Mick Deane, dying after he was shot in Cairo in 2013.

But not Bucha.

The Ramsay team - all five of them could have died there and then - but they got out alive saved by training, armour, and their experience.

Good luck too. Looking back at what happened on that Monday afternoon in very late February 2022 I still feel sick but believe it's right to ask our correspondents - those with the right training, right experience, right temperament, to risk their lives to bear witness to the brutality of totalitarian regimes. Eye-witness journalism. I salute those who try to see with their own eyes the truth for their professionalism and courage.

'A gut-turning moment'

'The accuracy of the fire was surprising,' was the laconic observation of *Sky News* camera operator Richie Mockler explaining what happened when gunmen, thought to be a saboteur Russian reconnaissance squad, ambushed *Sky's* chief correspondent Stuart Ramsay and his team as they drove in a Hyundai saloon rental car on a major road from Bucha to Kyiv about 20 minutes from the capital's centre. The gunmen fired hundreds of bullets.

Up close. One bullet hit Stuart in his leg. Richie was hit twice yet his body armour saved his life. The groupings of the bullets fired into the car's wind-screen bare out the precision of the ambush.

It took the team 22 hours to get to safety - I fidgeted, fretted, and bit badly my nails.

As a news boss it's a gut-turning moment when you first hear a team are in serious trouble often only moments after the incident begins and well before it's resolved. The news gyre stops turning. Things do fall apart. Yet the centre must hold, I told myself. The loneliness of leadership is striking, not for the first time, in 16 years at the helm.

Pause and reflect

When I first saw the video of the ambush three days later, I felt sick. Very sick. The rights and wrongs of broadcasting and publishing the video were discussed with my senior colleagues in the *Sky* newsroom in West London when the Ramsay team sent their report of the attack to London on the Thursday expecting it to run that very night. I decided to sleep on the video - to pause and reflect. Friday was tough but enjoyable.

After a lot of debate - at times punchy - both those who report the news from war zones and those who take big decisions in London - are passionate about *Sky's* journalism - two versions of Stuart's report ran on our television and digital platforms. A short piece I cut myself in an edit suite with the unruffled video tape editor Belinda Skudder - I hope the edit captured the precise ferocity of the Russian soldiers' attack - that aired on the Friday night bulletins along with a second longer version for Sunday evening produced by Jonathan Levy, the Director of News Gathering, that told the in-depth story of both the attack and the team's 22-hour ordeal and eventual escape. Leaders need to grasp calmly hard issues.

In an email to staff, I described the report as a 'hard watch' - a hard listen, too, in fact - with the crackle of the bullets, the team's desperate shouting and their heavy panting as they escape. In the end we decided to tell the story of what happened to show the sheer scale of the mayhem and violence meted out on the Ukrainian people and because it makes me angry the public don't understand the lengths journalists go to report the news.

A contemporary disagreement on platforms

After Friday's main evening editorial meeting, a smaller senior group gathered on Microsoft Teams, a little frayed, to discuss the planned rollout of material - the sort of discussions I've been part of for more than three decades. Straightforward. But then there was a distinctly contemporary disagreement which those of us who want to attract young audiences should remember.

Our head of digital output, Nick Sutton, a digital doyen, argued the video should also be published off-platform so it would be seen by *Sky News'* substantial audience on social platforms, both in the UK and internationally. He made the case that the audience there - particularly on *YouTube* - had shown huge interest in Ukraine coverage over the preceding week and that Stuart's report should be made available to them too. He also warned that if *Sky News* didn't publish it on social media, then others would rip off the TV broadcast and post it themselves. But the decision was made to restrict it just to *Sky's* own platforms. I should have listened harder to Nick. He didn't give up.

In the following hours, there was an overwhelmingly positive reaction to Stuart's reporting with many people commenting about how effectively it highlighted the reality of the situation on the ground and the risks faced by ordinary Ukrainians. By 7am on Saturday, the article had been read by more than 1.6m users, the video had been watched 1.1m times and *Sky News* had been the top trending subject on *Twitter*. Describing it as one of the most brave and powerful pieces of war reporting and camera work he had ever seen, the head of digital output made the case on Saturday morning for us to reconsider the decision not to publish off platform. It was agreed that it would be published on *YouTube, Snapchat, Facebook* and *TikTok* with advertising switched off. Nick's persistence paid off.

The lesson I learnt is that news organisations can't expect younger audiences to come to them. Later that morning, Prime Minister Boris Johnson tweeted that the courage of Stuart and his team was "astonishing to watch" and that they were "risking their lives to ensure that the truth is told".

In the following days, more than 3.5 million users had read the article and the video had been viewed more than 6 million times. (Note 1 below).

A *TikTok* war

This hot and cold war has thrown up complex editorial, ethical and logistical issues to balance the safety of our colleagues with need to report first-hand independently a significant story. News organisations have become much sharper at protecting their people - I recall the lack of training when I set out as an ITV producer to cover the Bosnian civil war. Thirty years on our audiences have changed too. This is a *TikTok* war. An interview we did with a lone soldier guarding a bridge in Kyiv has more than 30 million views. User-generated content is increasingly used in our coverage but only after it's being checked by our verification team. The flow of UGC has slowed as the war has gone on and people flee the fighting.

This is now the biggest refugee crisis in Europe since 1945. Heavy times.

'What would you pack in a light suitcase as you leave your home in a hurry?', I asked a colleague. 'Running shoes,' was his swift answer. I was initially frustrated by our own inability on screen to effectively use maps to explain to our digital and TV audiences the military tactics - maps explain why battles are lost and won. Now our big screen map routines are proving very popular with digital audiences especially on *YouTube* as they hunt for explanation and analysis.

Red ink

It had been a tricksy week that tested the news organisation and tested its leadership. And tested the mettle of a top-notch reporting team.

Ramsay's team had delivered big time. In red ink I highlight in my diary the professional and family moments that test me - done it for more than 30 years. Bucha is in red. Out of the blue a few days later I'm invited to a soothing dinner party where a British Kremlin watcher predicted Putin will be defeated - seemed unlikely at the time.

London's Brook Green looked a long way from Bucha.

Early on I headed for the hills of West Oxfordshire, worn yet wiser.

Notes

[1] The analytics:

15.3 total video views.

3.0m on *Sky* platform - short version: 2.6m views; long version: 315k

10.1m on *YouTube* - Short version: 5.5m; long version: 4.5m views. Breakdown of top countries - US: 2.6m; UK: 1.2m; Germany: 0.5m.

2.0m on *Facebook*

240k *TikTok* - short version: 41k; long version: 208k

4.1m unique users for article

3.6m on *Sky News* website and app

500k on *Apple News.*

[2] Some of this article first appeared in the Royal Television Society's March 2022 magazine '*Television*'.

About the contributor

John Ryley is the Head of Sky News and has been since 2006. He began his television career as a BBC Graduate News Trainee and went on to programme edit ITV's *News at Ten*. The Royal Television Society in 2021 gave John the Outstanding Contribution Award saying he had 'effected genuine change in our industry'.

From the frontline. Upfront and very dangerous

Alex Thomson of *Channel Four News* is battle hardened and a doyen of British TV news war reporting. He is truly the 'fireman's fireman' - twenty plus wars under his belt. Here on the Ukrainian war frontline he clearly outlines his hopes and fears

27 April 2022 Ukraine

War reporting: 80% logistics, 10% luck and 10% journalism. And sometimes, indeed oftentimes, the journalism manufactures the luck. All the luck. After more than 30 years of it and more than 20-odd wars (some of them exceedingly odd) it still feels like this is the constant ratio or at least something along these lines.

First logistics … well for a start you need a team so far as TV reporting goes. In our case Ukrainian driver and fixer; the all-important producer; multi-skiller who shoots, edits, sound records, feeds cut packages to London then sets up the live shot then, maybe, eats food. Skilled work, multi-skilled work.

Local knowledge and language being essential, hence the need for the driver and fixer. The real crown jewel is to locate and hire a Ukrainian journalist and in Slava we were blessed indeed. Surly, chain-smoking, rarely moved to smile, but with lightening ability to sense and deflect incoming bullshit at a 1000-mile range and a never-ending stream of "why don't we do this?" ideas.

He wrote recently saying our odyssey across his incredible country had been "the best trip of my career". Given he spent much of the time (correctly) convinced he was dealing with a complete clown in my case, I am alarmed to ponder what his worst trip was.

A driver might seem a luxury but not given the state of Ukrainian roads and the sheer distances to cover in a place bigger than the UK and France put together. In a month we drove the equivalent of London to Delhi.

That set-up in place - which is no mean feat - you then need transport: our trusty white van. Don't stick massive TV letters in gaffer tape to ID you as media in Ukraine. The Russian battle symbol on their tanks and heavy armour is also V. It wouldn't do to have any misunderstandings.

Accreditation: none - then no war for you

Then accreditation. Always, always accreditation, war in, war out. If people back home knew just how bloody difficult it really is even to get to where war is being fought they'd be astonished. Before the shooting comes accreditation and an army of Ukrainian soldiers ready to check your laminated military accreditation pass across the national road network dotted with sandbagged and concrete block checkpoints.

Lose that precious laminated military media ID and for you, my friend, the war is over. At these endless roadblocks they don't care so much about passports. Couldn't care less about Russian visa stamps. But that pass is your door ticket to war: access all areas.

Which gives the Ukrainians brilliant control of the media. Foul up and they can and do confiscate your press pass: game over!

A Dutch reporter decided to live steam a Russian missile strike on an oil installation in Odesa before the Ukrainian authorities had confirmed it. Back to Holland he went with a ban on any return for some years. That news ran through the foreign press corps across Ukraine with lightning speed and deep penetration.

'Ukrainian censorship?' Subtle

It goes further. The aftermath of a missile strike in Kyiv some weeks back was filmed by a score of International TV crews - *Channel 4 News* included - and to date this strategic hit by a Russian missile in the heart of the capital has never been mentioned. Still less reported. Or broadcast.

This is an astonishing feat of censorship in the age of the internet, of near instantaneous tweeting and so forth. It is not the only such example. A week or two later in Kharkiv much the same thing happened. Again. Zero reporting.

The Ukrainians have some profoundly effective controls over the media and message remarkably well stitched up. Why? Because everyone is paranoid about having their precious press passes confiscated if they mess up. Simple but stunningly effective.

Russia's lumbering dictatorship has to go to the messy lengths of murdering journalists; shutting down publications and now passing a law making the telling of truth punishable by up to fifteen years in prison. The Ukrainians have much subtler but, in some ways, just as effective methods of media control. That said, unlike Russia the Ukrainians here have a limited concern for the dissemination of strategic info helpful to their enemy.

'Russian censorship' Much less subtle

Russia, being a dictatorship, imposes total control of the message and media by force and violence. Broadly the Russians want to do anything they can to suppress the truth that this is war and they have invaded. Ukraine naturally wants that truth beamed around the world incessantly.

Iron-fisted and ham-fisted by turns, like all dictatorships, Moscow ensured entirely one-sided coverage of this war of course. One sided in a way largely favouring Ukraine. Areas under Russian occupation are a virtual no-go for independent reportage. Of course, the usual motley crew of handpicked stooges prepared to parrot the dictatorship line for domestic consumption and online, do get access and military embeds across Donbas and Luhansk.

There have been some rare exceptions to this rule.

To their great credit, A*l-Jazeera* did somehow manage a carefully controlled foray into Mariupol briefly, under Russian supervision. That has proved impossible for ITN and the BBC. Even our attempt to cover the early days of war from Moscow foundered because although the Russian dictatorship will give you a visa (for £246) it won't issue your press pass upon arrival. It is promised day after day, but it never actually comes. Therefore, you cannot work because sooner or later officials, police etc will ask for your press accreditation.

See - the old accreditation muscle being applied again as it always is.

Security advisor or controller?

The other logistic member of almost all journo teams is the security advisor. Almost always ex-military (See Ch 2 in this book). There to advise on how most safely to go about the business of filming organised industrial-scale mass killing and destruction using high explosives and bullets. I use the verb "advise" carefully. They are there to help you get where you want for what you want. They are not there to decide where you go. That distinction can blur and be stressed, but it remains vital.

Journalists and journalism must decide what we do and where we do it.

Your security advisor - and in my case the producer - both have to send daily risk assessments back to London proposing what we would like to do over the next 24 hours. We cannot move anywhere without informing London. Nor without its agreement. London is also tracking us electronically into the bargain.

It should come as no surprise that different news organisations have different levels of what they will tolerate by way of risk. Moreover, how the war looks from London is rarely, no, is never, the way it looks from on the ground. There are positives in this fact. And there are negatives.

Decisions on how close to get to 'bang-bang'

When you see some journalist getting right up among the shelling and the 'bang bang' this is invariably a combination of three factors.

First the decision of the reporter (and surely to God I hope) their entire team - unanimously- wanting to go to such a location. Second the permission of the Ukrainian Army or other official body to go to such a location. Third, the go-ahead from London/Paris/New York etc to do it.

In short, it doesn't just happen.

That said, in this war we have already lost colleagues and will lose more for sure. To some degree that is the nature of the work of course.

Sky's close call with death

To come upon the shot-up car of the *Sky News* team south of Irpin was a salutary experience. We sent stills of the bullet-riddled hire car back to colleagues at Sky. It might be of some use, we thought.

The video of that car being raked by automatic fire and the completely miraculous escape without serious injury to anybody in it, sent a shockwave through this relatively small industry and tiny war-reporting wing of it. (See Ch 1 in this book.)

I am unsure, but sense that incident has had a considerably chilling effect on the three factors listed above and thus the willingness of some UK newsrooms to sanction fishing trips up roads that look unpredictable or toward areas where shelling is known to happened daily. Over-cautious? Cavalier?

It is an abiding debate in every war I have covered.

My close call with death

But all this can only do so much. South of Chernihiv in northern Ukraine, the car in front of us hit an anti-tank mine one afternoon. The driver was killed instantly and his car was shredded. He'd driven on the verge for some reason that will never be known. Off the tarmac, in many areas, is absolutely no place to be in a vehicle.

Had we been a few seconds ahead the blast would have caught us too. No question.

Risk assessment will only get you so far in a place scattered with mines. In place where a missile can hit at any time. You can be as aware as you want about land mines. Those around you? That poor man just in front?

Drones can mean danger for journos

Moreover, technological advances in new gathering and war fighting have arrived dramatically in Ukraine. Ukraine has proved to be the war where the drone came of age on the battlefield. Turkish supplied attack drones in particular have made the tank look outdated, like a mobile reinforced steel coffin. (See Ch 16 in this book.)

So too, drone journalism has arrived on the battlefield on a big way. To some, a sparingly used artifice in news gathering, to others getting drone footage is a near obsession to get airborne and tell a truth that only birds recognise yet humans delight in.

The two do not mix in the war in Ukraine. Northwest of Kyiv, close to the frontlines of retreating Russian forces, I was astounded to see two journalists flying a drone. So much so that before I really knew it I found myself wandering over to them and saying this was a very bad idea. As in really bad. As in 'do you want to get us all killed here?'.

Just about three minutes after their precious tv airborne mission was complete, a shell duly smashed into the area, exploding a couple of hundred yards from where the droners had been. It was the only shell fired whilst we were there. Coincidence? Possibly, but drones are also weapons and it did absolutely not feel like coincidence that morning.

A few days later in Saltivka, a suburb of Kharkiv that is gutted by weeks of bombardment, another drone buzzed above us out of the blue. Because of the amount of shelling it was hard to hear. Military? Media? We did not wait around to find out. Nor did we bring a drone to Ukraine. On the whole I'd say the drones are best left in their boxes in a modern war zone where they are weapons as well as news gathering devices, a marriage made in the hell if our experience is anything to go by.

Clap for Ukraine in the UK

As I write this back in the UK I continue to be amazed at how this whole, awful war cuts through with people. British towns and villages fly Ukrainian flags. Friends open their houses to refugees.

Names burn into global and British consciousness in a way few other wars have achieved: Bucha … Mariupol … We all know we are at proxy war with Russia. In that, the dictator Putin and his marionette Lavrov are correct. It touches us in a way the break-up of Yugoslavia in the heart of Europe never did. Nor the long and lost war in Afghanistan where British lives were smashed and lost. Nor the complex, mutating war in Syria.

Ukraine is us, in a startling and brutal new way so few of us ever thought possible.

Not least that has dragged our journalism here into the position of first-draft evidence gathering for potential war crimes as never before. That is not necessarily the most comfortable place for a journalist to be. Not necessarily what journalism is in its first drafting of history. But like it or not, that is where we are.

Not a few reporters have felt perfectly comfortable going further and overtly accusing Russia outright of war crimes. In a rare reversal of this narrative, it was largely left to the *New York Times t*o consider evidence of Ukrainian atrocities as well.

From these initial recollections hot from the frontline the picture emerges then from Ukraine, of a startling blend of ageless, timeless dilemmas intrinsic to the craft of war reporting alongside startlingly new challenges to the simple/complex challenge is trying to tell it right.

About the contributor

Alex Thomson is a Presenter and Chief Correspondent, *Channel 4 News*. He has been with them since 1988 and is the longest serving journalist on the programme. Previously he worked for the BBC in Northern Ireland. He is multi-garlanded with industry awards.

Go east, young man. Follow the 31st Brigade

War reporting does not get more raw and first hand than this. Paul Kenyon of the BBC's _Panorama_ has now made three programmes since the Russian invasion. Here he follows a group of Russian killers, maybe war criminals, as they move from the North to the Eastern Front

In April 2022, cherry blossoms drifted across Kyiv's Shevchenko Park. Coffee stalls had reopened, pensioners played chess in the open air, and traffic hummed along the dappled boulevards unhindered by soldiers and roadblocks. The Russians had withdrawn from their six-week occupation in the northern suburbs, and residents were emerging for the first time since 24 Feb, venturing gingerly into the Spring sunshine to survey a city forever changed.

I had visited Kyiv on several occasions before, and was there at the start of the war, in the bitter cold of late winter, when the bombs first began to fall. I had a strange encounter back then. My film crew and I drove to Hostomel airport to investigate reports of a missile strike. It was the first day of the conflict. We came around the corner and found ourselves face to face with a unit of Russian soldiers. They crouched and made as if to shoot. They were the first Russians on the ground in Kyiv and we were lucky to get away with our lives.

During the days and weeks that followed, Hostomel, along with the neighbouring suburbs of Bucha and Irpin, became the epicentre of the Battle for Kyiv.

Return to Hostomel

When I returned to Kyiv in the Spring of 2022, with evidence of war crimes just beginning to emerge, the idea was to trace that unit of soldiers - the 31st Air Assault Brigade - and to investigate their behaviour towards the civilian population.

The nearest residential area to the airport is the newly-built Pokrovsky Estate, a collection of pale pink tower blocks fringed with freshly planted trees. We travelled there in the last week of April, past burnt-out tanks and destroyed buildings, and found the estate blackened by fire damage and punctured by multiple artillery rounds. We were soon approached by residents desperate to tell us what had happened. It was a rare moment in journalism; the realisation that many of these people had spoken to no one else about their experiences, that their stories were fresh and raw, and that what we found was likely to have long-lasting significance. We were taken to the fifth-floor apartment of a brave young woman called Alla. Every door along her corridor had been smashed, every home looted. The culprits had come across the fields from Hostomel Airport, on foot and in tanks. Alla told us how they had beaten her husband until he was coughing up blood. Did she know which unit was responsible? Alla's mother-in-law, Lybov, took us down to the cellars where the answer, she said, was written on the wall.

"I slept down here while they rampaged through the block", Lybov told me. "One of the soldiers was more approachable than the rest, and so I asked him the name of his unit." She had chalked his response across a door and the writing was still there: "The 31st Brigade."

Everyone we spoke to on the estate had been looted. Many had been beaten. All had had their mobile phones confiscated in order to stop them passing on information. Alla had managed, ingeniously, to keep hers by hiding it in the seam of her daughter's pink wellington boots. "I messaged my sister just once a day" she told me, "I sent just two words; "I'm alive"

We are the 31st

The 31st Brigade didn't just raid the Pokrovsky Estate. They took residence there, living in apartments while the residents were herded into cellars. They used it as a kind of barracks before heading off into neighbouring suburbs to fight. Their behaviour, it seems, deteriorated as they took heavy casualties during their failed attempts to enter Kyiv city centre.

I meet a man called Yuri. He is a veteran of the Soviet army, having fought in Afghanistan in the 1980s. Now retired, he's wiry and energetic, with determined features and piercing blue eyes. Yuri wants to take me for a drive, to show me what happened to him a week into the war.

He had been with the Mayor of Hostomel and a couple of friends, delivering food and medicine to the elderly. The Russians had been in occupation a week and supplies were already running low. It was difficult to move about at the time because the Russians were intimidating people on the streets. None of Yuri's group were in the military. None were armed. They were in a civilian vehicle. They hoped all would be okay.

As they drove past a waterway, they spotted a column of Russian vehicles on the other side. It was too late to turn around.

Suddenly there was a volley of gunfire and Yuri's best friend, Ivan, who was sitting beside him on the rear seat, slumped onto his lap. There was blood coming from the side of his head. He'd been hit, but he was still alive.

Immediately they sped along a back road, aiming for a medical centre. It was situated on the ground floor of the Pokrovsky Estate, beneath the blocks now occupied by the 31st Brigade.

As they came around a corner, there was a barrage of gunfire. Yuri leapt out of the vehicle pulling the injured Ivan behind him, and took cover beneath a mechanical digger. "Then they really started firing hard", he tells me. He leads me to the spot where it happened. There is broken glass and a metal fence riddled with bullet and shrapnel holes.

Death by Russian gunfire

"Where were the shots coming from?" I ask, and Yuri points to a bomb-damaged building on the Pokrovsky Estate about two hundred metres away.

The bursts of gunfire continued, and then the Russians seemed to become impatient and began to fire grenades at Yuri's position. By now it was getting dark. Ivan had died from his wounds. The Mayor was sprawled on the freezing earth, already injured from shrapnel. At some point the Mayor's phone rang. Yuri thinks it was the sound of the ringing tone that drew the next wave of gunfire. The Mayor was shot dead.

Yuri explains that he and the only other survivor, Taras, were crouching behind the digger with their backs against a high metal fence. Their only means of escape, they decided, was to dig beneath it. Using a knife and their bare hands, they scooped away the earth for more than an hour. They had to go deep, the fence had foundations. Eventually there was enough space to wriggle through. Even then, they hid on the other side for three days before summoning the courage to continue their journey home.

He's a tough man, is Yuri. He tells me all this with fierce intensity and when I probe too closely about how he felt seeing his friends killed in cold blood, he fixes his stare on the floor, composes himself, and responds formally with only a glint of moisture in his eyes.

On the face of it, this looks like a war crime; two unarmed civilians killed during what seems to have been an evening of sport for the Russian soldiers. The 31st was in control of the apartment blocks that day. Other units may have come and gone, but the 31st were in charge.

They have since been redeployed to the Eastern Front in Donbas, the scene of fierce fighting. It's where I needed to go next, to visit the frontline towns that lie in the path of the 31st Brigade today.

Heading East

I find myself in a Soviet-built sleeper, leaving at midnight from a blacked-out train station in Kyiv. The journey is all old-world bunks, steaming urns of tea, and guards with torches and whistles. The windows are the only clue that the country is at war - taped Blitz-style, blinds drawn to hide the cabin lights.

Myself and my BBC team pick up a van in Dnipro, the gateway to the east, where the atmosphere is highly charged. It's early May and air raid sirens wail throughout the day. A week earlier the airport had been hit hard, and no one's taking any chances.

The road out of the city to the east is almost empty. Just miles of arrow straight tarmac and plains of wheat. Every half an hour or so, we encounter check points controlled by twitchy young soldiers who demand passports and accreditation. Ukraine has imposed strict but understandable conditions on journalists. We are not allowed to film any Ukrainian military positions, nor can we film the immediate aftermath of a missile strike. The authorities insist we wait 24 hours after an attack, so as not to give away intelligence about casualties. A Dutch reporter was expelled from the country for allegedly failing to adhere to those rules.

After Hostomel, Donbas for the 31st?

As we enter Donbas, the fields are scarred with trenches that go on for miles. They are deep and fresh, and the diggers are still at work.

In the near-empty city of Slavyansk - a key strategic target for Moscow - the atmosphere is similar to that of Kyiv in those dark opening days of the war. Seventy per cent of the population has fled. Shops are closed. Sirens are incessant. Local officials have left. Soldiers look tight-faced and tense, and all around the sound of multiple rocket launchers. The day we arrive, I witness a Russian cruise missile attack against the main rail bridge connecting Slavyansk to the next settlement along.

The closest I can get to the front is a small town called Barvinkove. "One day it is safe", says our military escort, "the next day, crazy total war." Every street is laid with coils of barbed wire. Concrete slabs the size of juggernauts form chicane roadblocks. A rocket launcher fires a full, deafening barrage, and then speeds away to avoid retaliatory fire, its driver grinning and waving.

There is only one man on the street, a cyclist. I wave him down and ask if he knows about the war crimes committed against residents of northern Kyiv. Yes, he has seen the stories. "I've got cancer" he tells me, "so I'm not leaving. If they come I will hide and join the underground."

Why Donbas?

Donbas is a talismanic region for Putin. He cannot claim any kind of success in Ukraine without winning here. His forces already control around a half of it (Russian-backed separatists have controlled a third of Donbas since 2014) and although the Russian advance is slow, it is also determined and intense. What hope for those who remain in these war-torn towns and villages, awaiting the arrival of units like the 31st Air Assault Brigade and others who have redeployed east.

There are likely rogue soldiers among them, men who may have committed war crimes in Kyiv and are now fighting on the Eastern Front. They may well treat the remaining residents the same as they did in Hostomel, Bucha and Irpin. In the capital prosecutors have already begun examining evidence and collecting testimonies, but Donbas is unlikely to be free of its occupiers for many months and even years to come.

My journalistic takeaway

A large team is needed to make this type of programme. Ours included myself, producer/cameraman Nick Sturdee (who speaks Russian), fixer Taras Shumeyko, a High-Risk Advisor (former British paratrooper), two local drivers with two vans, and a backup team in London. Every stage of the journey was planned meticulously with the help of multiple intelligence sources and a constantly updating map showing the position of Russian troops. Journeys to frontline towns had to be arranged with the Ukrainian military.

Filming in this environment has to be quick and focused. There are rarely chances for a second take.

The expertise of a local fixer is paramount. They need to be able to plug into a network of contacts in order to get access, otherwise you will end up sitting in a hotel with lots of other journalists, effectively unable to move.

About the contributor

Paul Kenyon has spent thirty years working for the BBC, most recently in a freelance role. He reported for *Panorama* from the Ukraine War in 2014 and in 2022, and from the Libyan Civil War in 2011. He is the author of three books, two about Africa where he made several films between 2007 and 2014. He is the winner of an RTS specialist journalist of the year award and a BAFTA

From saboteurs to social media: Covering a new type of conflict

For reporters covering the invasion of Ukraine, Russia's unique brand of hybrid warfare required us to think again about how to cover conflict. But misinformation from Moscow required a new form of journalism to come to the fore too. Rohit Kachroo of ITV News explains

For a few moments I could have been fooled. It was 25 February 2022, a sunny Friday morning, when I tiptoed along the edge of a road on the banks of the Dnipro River in Kyiv with Maxim, our local producer. Before us, a jogger wearing AirPods pounded the narrow stretch of pavement, changing her path to dodge a tussle with an oncoming dog being loosely held by its owner who was staring at his phone. Behind the distracted dog-walker was a teenager on a scooter who slowed down to avoid the jogger, the puppy, its owner and, eventually, us. This felt so ordinary - the extreme normality of a group of strangers' mundane routines entwining ahead of a long weekend. But this would be the longest weekend.

Maxim and I were at work, but work was covering the invasion which had begun the day before, although looking around, you wouldn't always have known it. We were wearing body armour as we negotiated our way through the group of strangers. And as I turned back to my left, I was reminded of why we had stopped at this spot: perching behind a wall closer to the river were half a dozen soldiers with their firearms. It felt like we were looking at a split screen - one riverbank, two worlds. The troops had been sent here in response to fears that a so-called reconnaissance unit from the Russian military had been despatched into the city to prepare the ground for a forthcoming siege.

'Russian saboteurs'

It felt like an unfamiliar concept, but in this war the presence of so-called 'Russian saboteurs' - units of undercover agents working for the Russian intelligence agencies or military - heightened anxiety among the Ukrainian military. The well-founded fear of them by journalists as well as local soldiers was part of why this conflict was so different to others for reporters in the field. Over the coming weeks we would discover that troops manning checkpoints would feel jumpy wherever we went, wondering whether teams claiming to be journalists were Russian agents in disguise. And sometimes we would be cornered outside government buildings or pulled out of vehicles by suspicious soldiers who wanted to know that we were who we said we were.

Occasionally their starting point would be to assume that we were all liars, even when we produced our accreditation, until the point we made a compelling or particularly passionate argument. During the early days of the war, it didn't help that the 'TV' markings plastered across our vehicles in white tape to identify us as journalists, looked so similar to the letter 'V' painted on some Russian tanks. We couldn't have foreseen many of these challenges when we planned our assignment from London weeks earlier.

End of normalcy

Back on the riverbank, the dog, its owner, the runner, and the teenager on a scooter had disappeared by now. Their relaxed manner had been a contrast to the grave warnings about what would happen once Russia's invasion began - we were now almost thirty-six hours into it. A few weeks earlier, the Chairman of the US Joint Chiefs of Staff, General Mark Milley, had said Kyiv could fall within 72 hours of an invasion. Yet the Ukrainian soldiers we had stopped to film appeared to be acting out of an abundance of caution - there was no real evidence here that a battle for Kyiv had begun, as far as we could tell.

Then, with no further warning, gunfire erupted.

Ukrainian soldiers had spotted something. They were shooting at what they believed to be one of the notorious reconnaissance units. Maxim and I ducked behind a two-foot wall we had spotted earlier and identified as a potential hiding place, should we need one. We shared the cramped spot with an army commander who I filmed on my camera phone firing bullets - he broke away for a moment, looked at me, and whispered a warning: "SNIPER!" he said, indicating he had seen someone shooting towards us from across the river. The chaos grew. The rest of our team was thirty metres away, further along the river, taking cover close to our vehicle. They filmed Ukrainian troops backing away across a bridge in front of them against the sound of shooting and occasional explosions. The war had made itself visible in front of our eyes.

After five minutes of mayhem the shooting subsided, the scene cleared. The runners and dog walkers of the neighbourhood returned. Although within minutes we could see some people emerging from their homes nearby with suitcases and boxes as they decided now was the moment to escape the city.

War business: not as usual

This was an early lesson - a myth-shattering moment. Ukraine's nuclear neighbour had despatched a shadowy unit to fire across a river, perhaps in preparation for an attempt to overthrow the government. Even by the standards of modern warfare, this was not business as usual. It taught us that this war would not look like other conflicts. And to compound the challenges for journalists deployed here, reporters who had seen the wars in Iraq and Afghanistan through organised, formal military embeds would not have the same option here. And perhaps most difficult, with so much of the war being fought with artillery, in many places there would be no sign of a recognisable frontline.

Within a few minutes of our footage going online, an army of open-source investigators got in touch on Twitter asking me whether they had correctly identified our location. Here was another reminder that this was a different type of war for journalists. Over the previous weeks, alongside my colleague ITV News global security producer Dan Howells, we had used some of those same tools. Night after night we had reported on the build-up to an invasion by using geo-location techniques unavailable to reporters who covered previous wars or uprisings. Every day during the week before the invasion, we saw new videos being posted on *TikTok* and other social media platforms by civilians which appeared to show Russian tanks and troops on the move - mysteriously, some of the vehicles had the letter 'Z' emblazoned on them. We analysed and verified the footage and were able to prove that the military hardware we could see in the short clips was heading towards Ukraine, despite claims by the Kremlin that they were moving away. During the run up to the invasion, these investigative methods gave us confidence that we were not being 'spun' when Western governments talked about an invasion being highly likely.

New wars, new journalism

Russian misinformation combined with the need to scrutinise our own government had required a new form of journalism to come to the fore. But the stream of messages that followed the incident by the river showed that those techniques are available to armchair analysts too. Ukraine taught us that the gap had shrunk considerably between a reporter's tablet of stone sent from the field, and an analyst's tweet posted from an armchair. Important conflict reporting doesn't always have to happen from conflict zones.

Some of the storied journalists who have for years told younger generations that wars won't happen in the way they used to, were only partially correct. Tanks from invading countries on the streets of European cities are not a thing of the past after all. And although conflicts can be fought by drone operators and cyber attackers far away, the invasion of Ukraine has been both medieval and modern. For reporters covering it the lessons learned elsewhere taught us something - but not everything - required to cover this new type of conflict..

About the contributor

Rohit Kachroo is the Global Security Editor for *ITV News*, reporting on international affairs, national security, and counterterrorism both in the UK and around the world. He has won several awards, including from the Royal Television Society, for his reporting of ISIS. Rohit was previously based in Johannesburg for ITV News and *NBC News*, where, as Africa Correspondent, he covered the famine in East Africa, the death of Nelson Mandela and wars in Mali and Central Africa Republic.

Nothing is unthinkable: The new European disorder

Wars are not just about fighters and 'bang bang'. They are about ordinary people - the bereaved, the uprooted, the walking wounded whose scars may not be visible. BBC veteran foreign correspondent Orla Guerin picks through the detritus in Ukraine to uncover the lives forever changed by 24 February 2022

Exodus from Irpin

They came on foot, in an endless stream - trying to outpace the horrors behind them. Russian shells were laying waste to their hometown. There were young mothers with babes in arms, toddlers clutching toys, and the elderly moving as fast as their years would allow. Most were silent. Some were weeping. They picked their way hurriedly across a freezing river, balancing on jagged boulders and planks of wood.

It could have been flickering news reel footage from World War Two, but it was a scene from war in Europe in 2022. This was the exodus from a once comfortable commuter town called Irpin, at the edge of Kyiv. It was 7 March, twelve days after President Putin sent his tanks rolling across the border into democratic sovereign Ukraine. Months on few - except Ukrainians - still count the days.

"Everything is bombed," said Valentina, as she rushed past - a pensioner fleeing her home and her life with just a single bag over her shoulder. "There are no lights. There's been no electricity, no gas, and no internet for two to three days. People are sitting in the basements."

"It's hell, really hell," said Andrei, a thirty-something event planner, escaping with his pet poodle. "The Russian soldiers are bombing civilian houses. They are not fighting the army. They are fighting anyone. Tell everyone to close the skies, urgently. We need it."

Andrei's pleas for a no-fly zone went unanswered. And Irpin became a template for what was to come - a relentless assault on a city and its people, Russia's tactic of choice, honed in on Grozny and Aleppo.

War closing in

I arrived in Kyiv on a crisp winter's night in late January - a geo-political lifetime ago. The capital was picture-perfect - onion-domed churches shimmering in the moonlight, and elegant streets lined with glitzy shopfronts. But there were loud warnings from London and Washington that war was imminent.

Western intelligence - so discredited in the past - was on the money this time. This was an invasion foretold, despite Russia's constant refrain *"we have no plans to invade."*

On the drive from the airport, I was pulled back in time, to a previous visit to the city thirty years before. An independent Ukraine has just emerged from the ashes of the Soviet Union. What I remember from that time was a kaleidoscope of chaos, hope and possibility.

The Cold War was over. The world seemed safer, irrevocably so - perhaps because I was 23, with my foreign correspondent 'L plates' still on.

Fast forward to 2022, and a Russian leader - who cut his teeth in the KGB - was about to open a dark new chapter in Europe. At a stroke Vladimir Putin upended the established security order and then hinted he might go nuclear.

Unthinkable?

In the weeks that followed nothing seemed unthinkable.

Stepan's Story. Killed at two. My memento

Before his afternoon nap, Stepan asked for his new bed sheets which had stars on them. So, his mum is changing his bedding. "He ate well and went to bed and fell asleep," said his father Oleg Schpak, "and he never woke again. "

Two-year old Stepan was the victim of a possible war crime - an apparent Russian missile strike on his house in Novi Petrivtsi, North of Kyiv, in mid-March. It took twenty minutes to dig him out from under the rubble.

A few weeks later Oleg met me at the garden gate, still standing though the house wasn't. He walked me through the wreckage, pausing at the spot where Stepan was found. He was low spoken and shed no tears - his grief buried deep as shrapnel.

Disaster struck in broad daylight while Oleg was at work, but witnesses and survivors established the timeline.

"It was at 14.20pm," he said, giving the precise moment when his family of five was reduced to a family of four. "My elder son was in the furthest room. He was injured by the blast wave but not too badly. My wife and our three-month-old daughter were saved by the bedroom door. It protected them from the shrapnel. When my wife went to hospital she did not know, for a long time, that Stepan was dead".

41

Oleg's last sighting of his son was of his tiny broken body in the morgue. Now he has only his memories and the images of his phone. They show a blond-haired boy, with a sweet smile. In one photo Stepan is bundled up against the cold, with a toy shovel for clearing the snow. In another he's surrounded by an array of stuffed toys. "He could count to ten," Oleg says with pride, "and knew almost all the alphabet. He was lively, and well behaved."

Stepan's last days were full of fear, trapped inside, as the Russians made their failed push on the capital. 'He spent twenty days like a mole in a catacomb," said his father. "He understood that he could not turn on the lights. Like any little child he wanted to play. "

Oleg believes the war will last as long as President Putin does.

"While Putin is alive, he'll keep trying to take Ukraine," he said. "I don't understand why in hell he decided to send his troops here. To save people from what? From whom? There are no Nazis. This is a country where people lived freely."

As the invasion grinds on, Ukraine is gathering evidence and demanding accountability. Some Russian soldiers have already been tried for war crimes. It's unclear if anyone will ever be held to account for Stepan's death but by late May Ukraine's Chief prosecutor Iryna Venediktova said she was investigating almost 14,000 cases of alleged war crimes by the Russian invaders.

When we turned to go, Oleg put something into my palm - a small orange toy dog he had picked up from the ground. It belonged to Stepan. Perhaps he wanted to make sure I did not forget his beloved son. Covering wars over decades I have always hoped to come and go, returning home with no trace, mental or physical. (This of course is self-deception). But I could not discard this toy. I brought it back home, with my flak jacket and helmet. It now sits on my bookshelves - a permanent reminder of a golden child I never met, slaughtered in star-covered bedsheets. Whatever justice may come later, and whatever victory may be proclaimed (by either side), there is no reviving the dead.

The rush to arms, the lawyer with a rifle

He looked so out of place - like an extra miscast in a film.

With his gold-rimmed glasses, and stripy woollen hat, Yuri looked like he belonged in a hipster café. Instead, he was positioned behind a rifle sight at a breeze block checkpoint on the outskirts of Kyiv. When we arrived, he had just been handed a mug of steaming hot tea to combat the biting cold.

Yuri, like so many I met, was living by a new calendar. It had two time zones - *before* 24 February - when Russia unleashed its invasion at 5am - and *after*.

Before Yuri was a lawyer.

"I was representing my cases in a courtroom," he told me, "but if you don't think about it, and simply do what you have to do, it actually feels pretty normal already".

This was Day Six of the invasion, and he admitted he had never fired a gun before. I wondered if he was ready to pull the trigger.

"In the first two or three days after the invasion there was a lot of confusion," he said "and fear. Now after seeing what was done to our country, to our people, there is more anger. So yes, I am ready." In the early days of war, around 100,000 volunteers like Yuri rushed to arms joining territorial defence units. There were nurses, builders, carpenters, office workers - driven by war to shed their other skin.

Prepared to fight, ready to die

In the forest not far away I met another volunteer, sitting on the grass during a pause in a training session. Arthur was 32, and worried about the future for his four-year daughter Leia (he's a *Star Wars* fan).

"I am trying to prepare my will, while notaries are still working so that my money will be transferred to my family," he said. "This is a lottery, you may live, and you may not. It's Russian roulette," he said, an apt summary of the situation for him and for Ukraine. Arthur belonged to the Maidan generation - the young Ukrainians who spearheaded the pro-European revolution of 2014. He spent the years after that trying to reform and develop his country. His mood was sombre. So too his forecast. "What everyone is afraid of," he said "is that it's going to be a long war. It would be a battle of resources and resilience. How long will we live like this as a society, and how long will they?".

"But what I am afraid of is that out of weakness, out of despair, because they are losing this war, they will destroy it (Kyiv) as much as possible because of hate."

The Russians never made it to the capital - defeated by their own tactical blunders and the agile defenders of the city.

They had not reckoned with Ukrainian bravery and will to fight. (Neither had many Western governments.) But before Russian troops were forced to retreat, they terrorised, raped, and executed civilians in Irpin and the nearby town of Bucha - leaving bodies enough to fill mass graves.

And Ukrainians know President Putin's men may make another attempt at Kyiv, once the big battles are over in the East of Ukraine. Russian-backed separatists have been dug in there since 2014 when Moscow annexed the Crimean Peninsula. But Crimea is not enough for President Putin. He wants all of the old industrial heartland, the Donbas. If he cannot overrun Ukraine, he wants to dismember it.

Not wheat but charred bodies

Many here have already lost the world they knew, their quiet lives, and familiar comforts. Vitaly is one of those unmoored by war. His home is nestled among the fields outside Kyiv. But the verdant green landscape has been scared by war. I met the white-bearded 62 year old wandering among burn-out Russian tanks. He was one of the last civilians left in the area, clinging to the soil, despite the black smoke on the horizon, and the percussion of shelling. "We want to live, to grow wheat, and walk in the forests with our grandchildren, " he said, weeping. "Putin came and our children and grandchildren are dying. I can't leave this place. If needs be, I will die here. We don't this war and we don't want to die, but we *will* die for our land." In his grief and pain, he kicked at something in the grass. I glanced down to see the charred remains of a Russian soldier. "Putin killed them," he said. "He did it. Not us. He came to our home."

President Putin claims he attacked Ukraine to free its people from "Nazis" and oppression - an outlandish pretext for an illegal land grab. He has ignited the biggest war in Europe for seventy years, killed thousands of innocent Ukrainian civilians (and sacrificed countless of his own troops), caused millions to flee, and threatened global food security.

24 February 2022 reset the clock well beyond Ukraine. And in this dangerous new era, there is no unthinkable.

About the contributor

Orla Guerin MBE(Hon) is one of the BBC's most experienced foreign correspondents. She has reported from more than 80 countries, and been based in Johannesburg, Jerusalem, Rome, Cairo, Islamabad and Istanbul. During her decades in broadcasting she has covered wars in the Balkans, and the Middle East. Her work has won awards in Britain, the US, France, Italy and her native Ireland.

Exodus in reverse. Hitch-hiking to the frontline

When Russia invaded Ukraine, all airports in the country shut down, or came under attack. Crossing the border by land from neighbouring countries was the only way journalists could get in, and civilians could get out. Sometimes travel plans go smoothly, other times they are challenging. And every so often they become an adventure, characterised by the kindness of strangers, writes Dan Morgan

1 March 2022

'Good luck!'

With those parting words the young border guard handed me my passport and waved me through the Ukrainian side of the Siret border with Romania.

This was one week into Russia's all-out assault on cities and people across the country.

I had flown home to London a couple of days before the beginning of the war for my daughter's ninth birthday on one of the last commercial flights to leave the country. On my return, flying was no longer an option, and I was taking the land route in.

Like many of my colleagues I had spent weeks in Ukraine filming the lead up to the war which Western intelligence warned could start at any time.

Looking back their predictions had been very accurate and cut through the lies of Moscow's propaganda.

I'd been given a ride to the border with some colleagues at the German television station with whom I was working. We were supposed to drive over together, but their plans had changed at the last minute. I now found myself without transport and somehow needed to cross the country to meet my colleagues working out east.

Crossing the border

Watching the constant flow of people pouring out through the border, it was a spur of the moment decision to cross on foot.

I just needed to make it to the next town where my friend had found a driver who could take me as far as Vinnytsia.

Another friend also passed me the contact for a local activist from the university in Chernivitsi, about 70 kilometres from the border, where I could stay if I needed somewhere to sleep.

At the border, I saw aid organisations from countries across Europe, and armies of volunteers.

They were providing warm clothes, warm meals and tea and coffee to the hundreds of exhausted families making their way, often on foot through the wind and snow.

I saw mainly women and children, wrapped up in blankets and cold weather clothing, braving the bitter cold in a sea of bright neon jackets and colourful woolly hats.

Some carried pets, others dragged suitcases, a number came clutching plastic bags; some had nothing but the clothes on their back. Volunteers rushed to help, pushing pushchairs and guiding the elderly.

Amongst this exodus of people an Orthodox priest hobbled to and from the checkpoint carrying a large wooden cross over his hunched shoulders.

I watched as Romanian police and fire services ushered people onto waiting buses, from there they were taken to nearby hotels and shelters, many of which were letting people stay free of charge. It was a remarkable outpouring of goodwill in the face of collective outrage at Vladimir Putin's war.

Now pushing my way through the crowds on the Ukrainian side, pearls of sweat ran down my back as I carried my luggage, my equipment slung across my back and my body armour balancing in my arms.

'Excuse me, sorry, thank you'

'Excuse me, sorry, thank you,' I said again and again as I squeezed through the sea of people queuing from the other side. They were pressed up against each other, all leaving the country.

Only a handful of aid workers and I were going the other way.

In the chaos, queues of cars stretched into the horizon. Many Ukrainians had been waiting for days and nights to cross, exhausted and sleeping in their cars. In many of the windows, the Ukrainian word 'DETI': it means 'CHILDREN', written in large letters.

At this point millions of people had already left the country, mainly through Poland, driven from their homes, leaving cities like ghost towns in an apocalyptic movie.

Saying goodbye to the men

In scenes I'd see repeated in the coming weeks I watched as families embraced and cried as fathers said goodbye to their children, and wives took one last look at their husbands.

Unable to leave, these men had helped their families to safety at the border, now many would go on to fight.

Entire lives had been uprooted, most never really believed there would even be a war.

I saw children the same age as my daughters not wanting to let go of their fathers, fearing this hug might be their last.

I saw tears rolling down grown men's faces, and remember one young girl sat hunched over her suitcase clasping a toy rabbit, gazing speechless at the ground at the pieces of her broken heart.

After walking a few kilometres, watching all this unfold. I reached a petrol station where I paused for some rest.

Hitchhiking towards the front

Now I had to hitchhike.

It only took about three minutes of trying before a car stopped and a greying man, he must have been in his early seventies, waved me over.

'Chernivitz,' I said, and he gestured for me to get inside, before helping with my bags.

For the next hour we sat in understanding silence, I spoke no Ukrainian or Russian and he no English, so we sat listening to the radio.

A few times a minute the broadcast was interrupted by a pre-recorded message.

'Red Alert: aerial threat. Sirens sounding. Take cover now!' the message read in Ukrainian.

The warning was repeated over and over.

An hour or so later he dropped me at another petrol station where I had agreed to meet Sasha. One of the volunteers had passed me his number and he could take me as far as Vinnitsia.

Sasha drove what I think was a dark blue battered old Seat.

Once again communicating was difficult but I showed him my camera telling him I was a journalist.

Sasha called me correspondent in a Russian accent. I tried explaining I wasn't, but he had made up his mind. And he would repeat this at the dozens of checkpoints we passed along the road.

'British?'

'Journalist?'

I was asked each and every time, followed by a gesture of the hand to pass, and again and again those same words: 'Good luck'.

These checkpoints had appeared across the country, some manned by soldiers, others by volunteers. They used anything they could find for their defences. Tyres, sandbags, large pieces of steel and iron and concrete blocks. Smaller checkpoints leading away from the main road were often less professional, made using umbrellas, shopping carts, and old bicycles. Literally anything they could find.

Behind the fortifications dozens of Molotov cocktails were lined up along with spiked chains and rows of anti-tank mines that could be pulled across the road.

The soldiers had written messages to Putin and to the Russian soldiers and strung up mannequins from gallows as a warning.

Everywhere you looked they dug trenches, some of these men were armed with hunting rifles, others with AK47's.

The traffic in the opposite direction tailed back for kilometres at each checkpoint.

It felt like I was watching the entire country flee west.

Heading towards danger. Firemen

It's completely counter-intuitive, but that's generally the way reporting on wars works… we often head towards the danger, following black clouds of smoke or other signs of bad news.

Sasha listened to techno music and chain smoked one cigarette after the other the entire journey. Again, the music was frequently interrupted, by the red alert

By the time I finally reached Vinnytsia it was already dark and the roads had emptied.

There was a curfew in place, so most were indoors.

Arriving at the hotel, I paid Sasha the $100 US we had agreed. I wanted to give him more, but he refused.

Then he took off into the night, driving through the curfew, waving goodbye and saying, as you might have guessed, 'good luck' in broken English, cigarette still dangling from his lip.

With the whole country on the move, all hotels along the way were booked up but many had made space for people to sleep where they could.

The woman at reception led me to the back of the restaurant, through the unused kitchen and into what I presume was a small wedding hall.

Not a wedding room but a (free) dormitory

Mattresses and bedding covered the floors.

A few families sat on top of them.

Handing me a pillow, the receptionist told me I could sleep there for the night, and she said there was food upstairs in the building next door.

Sitting down for dinner I was brought some borscht and bread, and the owner came to speak to me, having heard a foreign journalist was there.

He had been giving people a bed to sleep and hot meal for free all week.

He said it was the least he could do, but with the sounds of war drawing closer he was in two minds now whether he should take his three children and leave the country.

He was worried and said things were getting worse.

Again, I offered to pay but was rejected.

He wouldn't take any money in these times.

Exhausted, I settled into bed.

Through the night families kept arriving but when I finally woke the next morning they had all gone.

Sergey, the owner, arranged a taxi that would take me on the next leg of my journey, handing me a packed lunch of chicken and potatoes for the road.

'Good luck!', he said as I left.

But it wasn't luck I experienced in the weeks to come while covering the war.

It was many of these random acts of kindness, from complete strangers, that kept me going.

About the contributor

Dan Morgan is an independent photojournalist working for multiple news outlets in Ukraine. He has filmed some of the most challenging stories of our time over a 15-year career. In most recent years he's covered Iraq, Syria, Afghanistan and Latin America. Dan has played a major role in the production of multiple award-winning documentaries and general news coverage for organisations around the world. His career has been defined by turning his lens to the human cost of war.

It's hard to be objective when your country's being bombed

The split life of Azad Safarov in the war zone: journalist by day, NGO founder helping children at night

For me the war started when I found myself throwing some clothes into a small suitcase, and packing my red, rented, VW Golf with that suitcase, a sleeping bag and one gas can with 10 litres of extra fuel.

I was leaving my favourite Kyiv for Lviv.

I was fleeing to the west.

There were many rumours that the Russians were already surrounding the capital. I was in a panic like millions of other people who couldn't believe that Russia would launch a full-scale invasion of Ukraine.

No, the war wasn't something unusual for me. I've worked on the front lines as a documentary filmmaker and journalist for foreign media since 2014, the beginning of Russia's hybrid war in the east.

I've spent more nights than I can count in trenches, I've come under fire, I've seen too many crippled and charred bodies, destroyed houses and bombed bridges.

But on 24 February 2022, I was in a panic because the thing I feared the most was becoming a Russian Prisoner of War.

There were rumours the Russian government had lists of politicians, journalists, pro-Ukrainian activists, and volunteers whom they would detain or simply kill first.

I found myself in several categories.

I've been working as a journalist in Ukraine for more than 15 years, and have made documentaries about the war in the east.

In 2019, together with my friend Lena Rozvadovska, we started a foundation *Voices of Children*, providing psychological and psychosocial assistance to children of war.

So I was the perfect candidate for these so-called 'shooting lists', lists of Ukrainians to be killed or sent to camps.

On the first day of the war I received dozens of messages from my friends urging me to leave Kyiv. Their fear spread to me, got into my head, and forced me to act.

My first response was to run.

I couldn't work as a journalist because I no longer thought about work, but about my and my family's safety.

I was very sorry to say goodbye to my team of foreign journalists, leave them behind and go to the west of the country alone.

I reassured myself that the Russians wouldn't touch them. They are not Ukrainians, they should have no problems with Russians, I thought.

Leaving Kyiv for Lviv

The first wave of guilt came as soon as I got into the car. It continued to grow as I left Kyiv.

It was the longest and hardest journey of my life.

The whole road was clogged with cars, and all the cars were packed with people, their pets and everyday things.

The traffic jam was dozens and dozens of kilometres long.

I had enough time to think, to realise that this is the reality, that this is not a dream, this is not a game.

I saw people picking up the last packets of crisps and nuts at petrol stations.

I saw people defecating on the side of the road, not even hiding it. Men, women, and children. It was as if the social norms and laws of order were gone, and the borders between people were forgotten.

I felt helpless as a journalist.

For the first time in my life I didn't want to record anything, I didn't want to film, I didn't want to stop and interview people.

My conscience as a citizen of Ukraine did not allow me as a journalist to show people in such miserable conditions.

Objectivity? Not possible

I have always been told that a journalist should be objective.

But how can you be objective when the enemy breaks into your house, kills your relatives, destroys your country? How can you remain just a journalist and cover events neutrally? There aren't any objective journalists left in Ukraine. We are all subjective.

We do our jobs and we risk our lives, while at the same time helping our country. Everyone does what they can.

The day the war started I left Kyiv feeling absolutely helpless and confused, with no understanding of what would happen to me and my country next.

But on that journey I also made a decision.

I decided I have to do what I do best, continue my work as a journalist and keep my NGO running.

Once I made that decision my panic settled, I started to breathe easier.

I had determined my personal frontline.

I drove to the town of Truskavets in the west of Ukraine. Usually, it takes seven or eight hours, it took me over two days.

I slept in the car, on the side of the road for four hours and then continued driving. Another journalist I was travelling with was afraid that we would come under fire and asked me not to stop. So, we drove and drove.

When we arrived I hugged my girlfriend, whom I had taken there a week before the war, and returned to my work as a journalist the next day.

Keeping *Voices of Children* going and growing

At the same time, I had to quickly expand *Voices of Children* to help as many families and children as possible. I couldn't give up one thing and focus on another. Both were important, and both required my attention, time and resources.

I knew a lot of people who wanted to tell their stories and I wanted others to see and understand what every family, every person, every child in Ukraine is going through.

I believe in journalism.

I believe in the way it can convey important information and make people act.

My connections with foreign journalists helped me publicise the need for psychological assistance to children of war. *Sky News, ABC News, BBC News, the New York Times, Esquire, Forbes,* and other international media started writing about us, and suddenly it was global.

We began to receive donations from all over the world. The United States, Britain, Germany, France, Hong Kong, and so on. The NGO, which in previous years had a budget of 30-40,000 euros, grew to a budget of three to four million euros in just a few weeks.

But to do it all was difficult, really difficult.

Prior to Russia's full-scale invasion of Ukraine, I worked for only one team of foreign journalists. When the war started the number grew to six teams at once.

I had to find them fixers and translators, get them accreditation, and try help protect them from the dangers of working on the frontline.

At the same time my NGO had to start doing things we had never done before, like evacuating families from the war zone.

We had to find them shelter in the west, buy them food, clothes, and other necessities just to survive.

We couldn't say, 'oh, I'm sorry, we only provide psychological help, try get out of hell yourselves, and when you're safe, our psychologists will take care of you'.

No, we couldn't say that.

So, during the day, I worked as a journalist. And at night I worked as the co-founder of an NGO, using all resources available to coordinate the evacuation of people and the provision of humanitarian assistance.

While others were resting or sleeping, I interviewed candidates to work with *Voices of Children* all through the night, recruiting qualified people to help us quickly expand the range of our activities.

As a direct result we now provide thousands of families with psychological and humanitarian assistance every month and *Voices of Children* now has dozens of centres throughout the west of Ukraine, more than 70 psychologists and about 30 staff, some of whom work from bomb shelters.

We have received support from the stars-Madonna, Oprah Winfrey, and Ellen DeGeneres. We have been approached by *UNICEF, Caritas,* and *Lumos* for cooperation. And all of this has happened in just a couple of months.

We don't have a business plan for five years, we don't even have a business plan for one year. It is difficult for us to plan our lives even for one week. We just do our job every day.

On the first day of the war I hurried to Lviv, to the west of Ukraine, to escape the Russians.

Today, on the 100th day of the war, I am writing this on the way to the east of Ukraine, to Kharkiv, which is still shelled every day.

I was born in Azerbaijan, and in the 1990s my family fled the Nagorno-Karabakh war to peaceful Ukraine. But as it turns out sometimes you can't escape war.

There is no point in running away, there is no point in being afraid.

I'm in too much of a hurry to tell the world all the important stories. And I am in a hurry to keep building the foundation, to make sure it's working to save thousands of children, even without me.

About the contributor

Azad Safarov is an award-winning filmmaker and Ukrainian journalist. He is also the co-founder of the Voices of Children Foundation, an NGO that provides psychological support to children on the frontline. His latest film documents the lives of children living in an orphanage in Eastern Ukraine. The film, 'A House Made of Splinters', recently won an award at the prestigious Sundance Film Festival.

The television war. Ukraine needs the media to keep delivering their message

Jim White is the doyen of football reporters. He plies his trade in the *Daily Telegraph*. But off-piste he looks at the British TV coverage of the war and argues the Ukrainians need the media to keep their war in the foreground and the weapons coming

On the evening of Tuesday 31 May, Reeta Chakrabarti was no longer, as she had so often over the previous three months, presenting the BBC ten o'clock news from atop a rooftop in Kyiv, a golden onion-domed tower glittering behind her. Rather, in the background as she delivered the headlines was Buckingham Palace decorated in projected pictures of the monarch. The Queen's jubilee pageant was now top of the running order, replete with tales of duty, service and care-in-the-community royalists camping out for days on the Mall to secure their position to watch it all go by.

Ninety-eight days since Russia invaded Ukraine and the war had slipped way down the news running order, to the point it was not mentioned on the BBC's flagship bulletin until the fourth story in. The slippage had been steady and unrelenting: from the only story on the agenda for the first few weeks of the invasion, Ukraine had, as the war staggered on, been overtaken by Partygate, by the cost of living crisis, by the windfall tax, by tales of the gathering uselessness of our police, by stories of the queues at Manchester airport, and of yet another ghastly school shooting in the US.

News is what news makes it

It happens. News is made up of what those in positions of editorial responsibility deem to be significant. More to the point, it is centred on where they decide to dispatch reporters. To update the old proverb about a tree falling in a forest, if Russian ordnance lands alongside a Ukrainian trench and Orla Guerin is not on hand to record it, then as far as the news is concerned, did it ever happen?

Things change. Other stories grab the attention, the scale of the coverage dependent on the judgement of news editors. This is what so infuriated many a stop-the-war-favouring poster child on social media when Ukraine was first attacked in February. Unable to portray the conflict as the consequence of Western aggression, they felt obliged instead to cast the media response to it as institutionally racist. The ubiquitous coverage of the war, they suggested, was because those caught up in it were white Europeans. What about what is going on in Yemen? There was never the same attention paid to that was there? Why were wars involving brown and black people being ignored?

Which is fundamentally to misunderstand that what makes it on to the nightly bulletins - particularly the news from elsewhere - is inevitably selective. It has to be. There is too much going on for it all to be recorded. For a while Ukraine was everything, just as Afghanistan was before it or as Lebanon was for a day or two when that grain silo exploded. Now it is not. Things move on. This is what news is: new. Ukraine is becoming old.

Has the UK lost interest in the Ukraine?

In Kyiv, they might legitimately wonder why the British interest in their awful predicament has waned. Why is it Clive Myrie is now reporting on Jubilee matters instead of delivering breathless nightly bulletins in a double act with Lyse Doucet while dressed in a flak jacket? It is not as if the Russian destruction of their country has diminished. The Donbas is still being systematically flattened. Kharkiv is still under the same awful bombardment. The Kremlin remains as unhinged in its ambitions as it ever was.

The truth is, Ukraine needs the war to be in the news.

It needs to influence public opinion in the west to ensure pressure is put on politicians to accelerate assistance. The best way for that to happen is on the nightly news. It is Jeremy Bowen's reports from places raped and pillaged by Russian troops that insist weapons must be dispatched. The bad news for them is that, just as the Russians are making slow but steady advances in the east of the country, here is the war disappearing from our collective consciousness, soon to be relegated to the 'and finally' slot.

Even *Ukrainecast,* the excellent BBC podcast hosted by Gabriel Gatehouse and Victoria Derbyshire, set up in February to ensure those interested in the war could be thoroughly and regularly updated, is under threat of being downgraded from a daily service to a couple of times a week.

Using the Western media

Ukraine's leaders have been quite brilliant at utilising the western media to state their case. President Volodymyr Zelenskyy has led from the top in his welcome embrace of foreign reporters. He has been as often seen interviewed on news bulletins as he has addressing foreign parliaments. Open, accommodating, hospitable, he will talk to anyone. And every time he does, the message is the same: we are fighting for you but the only way we can fight effectively is if you send us more weapons.

Across Ukraine everyone from town mayors to military commanders have followed his lead. Any reticence about giving away secrets has been put aside in order to fight the war on the second front: public relations. There is a reason Bowen was able to get into Bucha in time to send that bone-chilling dispatch of bodies lying in the street: the Ukrainian authorities gave him access. The result was one of the bleakest reports of the war, his astonishing footage doing more to challenge American and German reticence in supplying effective armaments than any diplomatic appeal.

The Russian media black hole

By contrast the Russians have singularly failed to influence western media thinking. Professor Tim Hayward, the Edinburgh academic who was accused in parliament of spreading Russian propaganda, has a point: we are not seeing anything from the other side. Beyond the occasional nonsensical comment from a Kremlin press officer, everything is through the lens of the Ukrainians. All we know about the Russians is from the brilliant BBC Moscow editor Steve Rosenberg, standing bravely in Red Square, delivering his reports about shouty Kremlin mouthpiece television hosts pumping out the ludicrous claims of liberating Ukrainians from the 'Nazis'. There are no *Sky News* reporters embedded with the invading forces. All we see of Russians are their tanks being blown up by British-supplied shoulder held rocket launchers or CCTV footage of their soldiers murdering civilians. There is no balance in the reporting.

This, though, is not the fault of the BBC, ITV or *Sky*. The Kremlin has cast its assault as a defence of Russian values against Western aggression, as us against them. In order to demonstrate its superiority, it doesn't need any cooperation. The image of an outgoing, expansive, internationalist Russia that they wanted to project when they hosted the World Cup just four years ago is no longer in evidence. It has been replaced by a deliberately inward-looking brutalist nationalism.

Keeping interest going on Ukraine. Samples from British TV

But if Ukraine's leaders are so adept at persuading the western media to see things from their point of view, how do they maintain the process as interest inevitably wanes? How do they stop us from getting bored and moving on? The answer was there in the three reports on the BBC, ITV and *Channel 4 news* that did go out on the evening of 31 May. They were all very different, filmed in different parts of the Ukraine. But they all focused on the consequence on individuals of the continuing mayhem. And more to the point, all of them were entirely dependent on cooperation from the Ukrainians.

On the *BBC*, the Kyiv correspondent James Waterhouse brought us a piece about the appalling treatment of Ukrainian prisoners by the Russians. He spoke to a fighter who had been injured in Mariupol, captured, and taken to Russia. There he had been treated with scant regard, respect, or humanity. He had been, it was clear, brutalised for the crime of being Ukrainian. Now back recovering in a Kyiv hospital after a prisoner swap, he was happy to tell his story to the BBC. And it was a grim one.

Likewise, on ITV Lucy Watson had a compelling story of Ukrainian children who had disappeared from areas occupied by the Russians, whole families gone missing. It was the human consequence of war. Meanwhile on *Channel 4 News*, Cathy Newman had a fascinating piece about how British aid workers in Ukraine were being targeted by Russian disinformation trolls claiming they were there not for humanitarian reasons, but to fight. That is what Russians do in war: lie, lie and lie again.

All three pieces provided persuasive argument against the growing belief among western politicians that the only way to end this war is to allow some sort of accommodation in which the Russians continue to occupy the east of Ukraine. Here was chilling evidence that the Russians are treating the population of the areas they have occupied with contempt.

So what is to be done?

The next night on *Channel 4 News* Paraic O'Brien was on hand to tell us. He had travelled to the Ukrainian front line out in the Donbas to find out what difference to the war would come from President Biden's announcement - made via his article published in the *Washington Post* - that the US would now supply the Ukrainians with sophisticated, long-range artillery. Sardonically pointing out that he had rarely encountered such an enthusiastic response to a newspaper op-ed column, O'Brien interviewed an officer who explained such weaponry was vital if Ukraine was to resist the Russian assault, stop them further brutalising his nation. But in order to make that difference, O'Brien was told, the weapons had to be got to the front line as soon as possible. Any delay would be self-destructive. Speed was of the essence.

Message delivered.

About the contributor

Jim White's latest book, *Red on Red*, an investigation of the history and wider social consequence of the Liverpool v Manchester United rivalry written in conjunction with the BBC's chief football writer Phil McNulty, is published by HarperNorth.

Still whooping it up with the war junkies

Andrew Beck offers a close reading of UK media reporting on the first one hundred days of the Ukrainian conflict. He argues that, although the war witnessed the move from broadcasting to digital, reporting remained distinctly old-fashioned in its themes and analysis

Come February 2022 there was a palpable sense of anticipation in British news media. Almost wrongfooted by the war's false dawn there was an equally palpable sense of relief once the tanks finally rolled in and the missiles started flying in Ukraine. Whilst there has never been a time since 1945 when there wasn't some kind of war raging in some part of the world, because it was on European soil with Russia as the aggressor, this looked like the big one. The shame here is that a novel war has been subjected to a stale old narrative.

Interviewed by Hunter S Thompson in Saigon in May 1975 *Newsweek*'s Nick Profit pointed to the perilous appeal of reporting the Vietnam war: "This is my third or fourth war […] and so you find yourself doing stupid things. You find yourself standing around in the open when you should be grovelling on your fucking face someplace" (Thompson, 1990: 187). Whilst contemporary news managers keep tighter control over reporters in the field the temptation to behave in a maverick fashion is still there. And while allowing that every young war reporter 'has got to do their first war assignment at some stage' in March the BBC's interim Director of News Jonathan Munro said he did his best to curb risky ambitions and appealed to other broadcasters to boycott ''cavalier' journalists who might have gone to Ukraine to make their name' (Burrell, 2022a).

Speaking in Oxford in May (see Prelude in this book) BBC World Affairs editor John Simpson felt the BBC's Ukraine coverage had been 'the polar opposite of its coverage of the fall of Kabul', that is, they did not miss the story. This desire to do the right thing this time led them to 'throw money, talent, quality' at Ukraine. Middle East editor Jeremy Bowen was drafted in, obvious trouble-shooters such as

Lyse Doucet were sent there, and many London-based anchors such as Ben Brown, Rita Chakrabarti, Clive Myrie, and Nick Robinson did tours of duty hosting live programmes from Kyiv. In his personal hall of Ukraine reporting fame Simpson singled out *The Independent*'s Kim Sengupta , felt the *Daily Mail* coverage had been very good, that ITN had been excellent, and that *Sky News* had been very good.

Almost overtaken by the accelerated pace of live reporting, 'mostly accessed by phone' (Munro), there was little time for any reporters to reflect on what was being witnessed or to slowly think through the issues raised by what was being reported. Despite this they were constantly being asked to do just that. And this led to a strong and consistent focus on the misery of the war, and to the reproduction of twentieth-century truisms about how the world lined up in terms of Ukraine: a veritably Manichean worldview.

"And, Laura, you must be hearing some heart-breaking stories from there" (Caroline Wyatt)

In terms of misery the lead para of Taz Ali's 25 April piece for the *i* is a sound example: 'As Christians in Ukraine celebrated Orthodox Easter Sunday yesterday, there was no end in sight to a war that has killed thousands of people, uprooted millions more and reduced cities to rubble'. Misery is piled on misery until he reports 'The governor of Ukraine's Donetsk region said two children were killed yesterday in shelling by Russian forces, as he urged people to evacuate areas near the fighting'. Further detail is then offered: 'Pavlo Kyrylenko said the girls, aged five and 14, died after the building they lived in was destroyed'.

The conflict's gruesome realities led reporters to offer almost verbatim transcripts of the first war crimes trial. Covered by both the *i*'s Victoria Craw and *The Guardian*'s Lorenzo Tondo the trial concluded with Vadim Shishimarin, 21, being found guilty of killing 62-year-old Oleksander Shelipov in the North Eastern Ukraine village of Chupakhivka. Tondo reports that Shishimarin said he 'was nervous about what was going on' and 'didn't want to kill' Shelipov. He then reports how Ukrainian prosecutor Andriy Syniuk dramatised this for the court: "Could he have stepped out of the car and expropriated the phone of the victim. Yes he could. Could he just make one shot? Yes he could. But instead, he killed a citizen of Ukraine".

The lead para for Isabella Bengoechea's 5 May *i* piece said it all: 'Women and minorities in Ukraine are being disproportionately affected by the way amid claims of sexual and domestic violence, human trafficking, a growing burden of care, and lack of food and vital medicine, a UN report has found'.

In a 27 April *i* report Sky News' Mark Austin, almost permanently installed in Ukraine, offered similar detail and commentary: 'What we found in Saltivka, a north-eastern suburb, was heart breaking'. And in Kharkiv he found more misery: 'Rocket fire and shelling several times a day causes untold damage here - all slowly burn away the fabric of a community, destroying the infrastructure, demoralising the people'.

War, and war reporting, is older than the hills. Barely a book of the *Old Testament* lacks reports of war. The *Odyssey* starts in the aftermath of Troy's bloody sacking. Odysseus kills the Cyclops by putting a rod right through his eye. Penelope's suitors are brutally murdered by Odysseus and Telemachus. Brutal military behaviour was satirised by Tacitus. That satire was updated in the 'From Here to Eternity' section of William S Burroughs' *Exterminator!*: 'Old Sarge bellows from here to eternity WHAT THE BLOODY FUCKING HELL ARE CIVILIANS FOR? SOLDIERS PAY' (Burroughs, 1974: 89). Of course this war is appalling, of course the targeting of civilians is grotesque, but as the refrain goes in Ishmael Reed's poem: 'Well this is war / and in a war such things happen' (Reed, 2007: 355-359).

"Today President Putin will use Russia's past to justify his present" (Jenny Hill)

Before hostilities broke out the sides were clearly and definitively marked out. Complex twenty-first century geopolitics were reduced to the simplistic nostrums of the Cold War. The Big Man Theory of history ruled: Putin was an evil, Communist dictator, and Zelenskyy was an aggrieved innocent. Interviewed for BBC Radio 4's *Feedback* programme on 20 May 2022, Jonathan Beale, the BBC's Defence Correspondent asserted that 'There are clear lies from the Russian side'. The evidence for this was 'They've lied about killing a person in Britain'. This was echoed by Steve Rosenberg, *BBC News* Russia Editor, responding to Russia Federation ambassador to the UK Andrei Kelin's answers to Clive Myrie in his lengthy and polite interview on BBC1's 29 May *Sunday Morning* programme: 'We've been hearing this for years […] This is the Kremlin narrative. We heard it after the Salisbury poisonings'. Dissenting views were few and far between. John Simpson did concede that 'Ronald Reagan wasn't in the least presidential but he knew how to *act* like a president'. Likewise Zelenskyy. And *Sky News'* director of newsgathering Jonathan Levy pointed out that Zelenskyy is 'a very adroit communicator' who makes 'good use of social media' (in Burrell, 2022b).

"It was a reminder that the world has their [Ukraine's] back" (Lyse Doucet)

In think-pieces for *i* Ian Birrell and Hamish McRae summed up this Manichean view of the Ukraine war. Invoking both Samuel Huntington and Matthew Arnold Birrell proclaimed this to be 'a clash of civilisations'. This was a 'seismic struggle of our time between autocracy and democracy' (Birrell, 2022). Begging the question of India and China's developed status Hamish McRae argued that 'It is hard to see the US or the EU accepting for long a situation where India and China benefit from cheap energy from Russia while the developed world pays much more'. He concluded that 'in the longer run there is a risk that the world will gradually divide into two trading blocs: the West vs the rest' (McRae, 2022).

"A war of the narrative" (Jonathan Beale)

War reporting fatigue set in early in the conflict. By 26 May Ukraine reporting had been pushed back to page 20 of the *i*, just ahead of editorial and commentary. Despite being consistently trailed as a make-or-break event for Putin (he must be able to demonstrate significant gains, significant victories) British TV news' coverage of the Moscow's annual Victory Parade on 9 May was less than fulsome. While BBC1 and *Sky News* took live feeds of the parade *ITV* interviewed Marco Pierre White, *GB News* discussed the Northern Ireland stalemate and Beergate, and *TalkTV* stuck with the Northern Ireland stalemate. Framed by Moscow correspondent Jenny Hill's scene-setting on BBC1 Security correspondent Frank Gardner offered commentary on and decoding of Putin's speech: it was short, he had a heavy blanket on his lap, and the air force display was cancelled due to bad weather. By 08:10 the programme BBC1 cut back to Northern Ireland while *Sky* stayed in Red Square. Only *Sky* ran Putin's speech live and uninterrupted. By 08:17 ITV ran Putin live with no onscreen translation but with commentary and editorialising.

British news media has consistently presented the Ukraine war as a tired reprise of the Cold War. This story has even been stretched to encompass World War II. If nothing else that has granted a scintilla of truth to Prime Minister Johnson's very frequent and very public rhetoric about his status as Churchill's successor. Unprecedented numbers of British media organisations have sent brave men and women into the Ukraine theatre of war. Many have risked their lives to broadcast live in dangerous and dispiriting conditions. It would be a shame if all the British public took away from this reporting was this rehash of Big Men, Autocratic Communism vs Democracy, misery, and petty point-scoring: a narrative unfit for this war and this time.

References

Taz Ali (2022) 'Russia accused of trying to 'finish off' plant guards', *i*, Monday 25 April.

Mark Austin (2022) 'Eyewitness journalism has never been more vital', *i*, Wednesday 27 April.

Isabella Bengoechea (2022) 'Women and minorities 'hit most by war'', *i*, Thursday 5 May.

Ian Birrell (2022) 'This is a clash of civilisation', London: *i*, Monday 25 April.

Ian Burrell (2022a) 'In the Ukraine war, digital media comes of age - and the BBC proves its worth', *i*, Monday 28 March.

Ian Burrell (2022b) 'The war in Ukraine is also being fought on the battlefield of propaganda', *i*, Monday 16 May.

William S Burroughs (1974) *Exterminator!*, London: Calder & Boyars.

Victoria Craw (2022) 'Ukraine jails soldier for crimes', *i*, Tuesday 24 May.

Hamish McRae (2022) 'How war could split the world in two', *i*, Thursday 5 May.

Ishmael Reed (2007) 'In a war such things happen', in *New And Collected Poems 1964-2007*, New York: Thunder's Mouth Press. Reed performs this poem in a musical setting on the March 2006 American Clavé Records release *Bad Mouth* by Conjure.

Hunter S Thompson (1975) 'Whooping it up with the war junkies' in Thompson (1990) *Songs of The Doomed*, New York: Simon & Schuster.

Lorenzo Tondo (2022) 'War crimes tank chief apologises for killing of civilian', *The Guardian*, Saturday 21 May.

About the contributor

Andrew Beck worked in UK secondary, further, and higher education for forty-two years, lastly as International Partnership Manager for Coventry University's Faculty of Arts and Humanities. He is the author of several well received, best-selling texts on communication and media. Although retired from full-time work he continues to teach at and advise international universities, as well as researching and writing on a wide range of communication, design, and media topics.

Captain Semenyuk. One Ukrainian, several wars

Kim Sengupta is a doyen of the newspaper war reporters. He has sent dispatches to the *Independent* from Ukraine for nigh on a decade. This is his latest on the latest war

The scenes of carnage outside Kyiv and Kharkiv were miniatures of the destruction we saw on the road to Basra and outside Benghazi. There the forces of Saddam Hussein and Muammar Gaddafi were caught in the open and pulverised by Western aircraft.

What happened in Iraq and Libya were bloody examples of the lethal impact first-world armed forces can unleash on weaker states. The Russian losses in Ukraine, the twisted metal and charred bodies of soldiers trapped in their armoured vehicles, however, was grim testimony of how a superpower has failed to impose regime change on a smaller country despite military might.

It has been extraordinary experience to witness this war which is reshaping modern history in a way comparable with the fall of the Berlin Wall and the 9/11 attacks and their aftermaths. It has also been a war unexpected and unpredictable in the way it had begun and unfolded, and remains unpredictable on how it will end.

In the beginning

On the early morning of 24 February, when we were in Kyiv experiencing the first Russian missile strikes, it seemed it would only be a matter of time before the capital fell. Ukrainian air defences managed to shoot down a large number of incoming missiles - but others got through, hitting apartment blocks, destroying homes, killing and wounding people.

Russian raiding parties repeatedly tried to get into the city. They were repulsed in firefights. It was claimed that infiltrators, including a team of Chechens, were in the capital to murder President Zelenskyy and members of his government: we saw the dead bodies of the "assassins".

A 40-mile-long Russian military convoy headed our way. A terrible threat awaited us, warned western politicians and military experts. The Ukrainian capital would be razed and left like Grozny after the Chechen war 20 years ago. And, as Moscow's forces edged closer to within 20 miles of the city centre, that seemed to be a distinct possibility.

I went to Kharkiv to find it under ceaseless missile, artillery and air strikes. The Russians had attempted to storm the city a number of times and failed. They were now destroying Ukraine's second city with long-range fire.

Kharkiv before and after the Russian bombardment

It was expected that the Kremlin would make a determined effort to take over the city in which 74 per cent of the 1.4 million inhabitants were Russian-speaking with supposedly divided loyalties.

On a visit to Kharkiv a month before the war, one resident, Kiril Semenov had stopped me to angrily declare "it is unthinkable for me and my friends to pick up a gun and start fighting our Russian brothers. We have lived together all our lives and now the Americans, Nato, are trying to turn us into enemies and start a bloodbath".

Mr Semenov, I found now that the conflict had started, had not picked up a gun, but he was part of a citizens' group distributing food to Ukrainian forces. "Nothing justifies this kind of bombardment, the killing of ordinary people, like those who lived in that building," he said pointing at the wreckage of a 10-storey residential block in the district where eight people had died in shelling. "Putin has bombed us into realising how Ukrainian we are."

A significant proportion of the population was living underground in the Metro system for safety. Emerging to buy food or collect items from homes damaged and uninhabitable, was dangerous. We saw a queue outside a supermarket getting hit by a rocket, killing, among others, an elderly woman who had come from one of the metro shelters.

Ukraine fights back. Horrors emerge

Yet slowly, against the odds, amid much bloodshed, the tide turned. The Russian forces were driven out of the north around Kyiv and then from around Kharkiv. For the first time, it seemed that Ukraine would survive Vladimir Putin.

Evidence of war crimes emerged as the Russians retreated, of murder torture and rape; victims in mass graves and simply dumped in streets: of looting and arson in homes, schools, offices and factories. These atrocities, we discovered, had taken place in a host of places - Bucha, Irpin and Cherniev and Hostomel.

In Bucha, which has become an emblem of what happened, we found the dead, some of those killed by the Russians had their hands tied behind their backs; some had been hooded with bullet holes in the back of the heads.

"They were left to rot after they died, as if they were bags of rubbish," said Dimitrou Zamohylny in Vokzalnaya Street. "In that time flocks of crows sat on the bodies, pecking out and eating eyes, we have descended into hell".

There were still bodies left in houses. One was that of 89-year-old Alla Minorava, lying on her bed, with bloodstains on her arms. She died on 25 March. Russian soldiers who had taken over her house told neighbours they had shot her.

Mounds of brown earth were piled up over a 45 feet long pit into which corpses in black plastic bags have been flung behind the Church of St Andrew and Pyervozvannoho All Saints. Up to 300 bodies were said to be buried there. Some of the bags have split, with legs and arms protruding. Limbs have broken free among the buried, rising up from the soil; a palm was cupped as if in supplication.

Ukrainian soldiers, laid out bodies of dead Russian soldiers, caught in an ambush on the outskirts of the town,. Nicolai Semenyuk, a captain in a volunteer unit, said as he watched "I don't feel any pity for them, they behaved like savages. You have seen what they have done here: the killings, the rapes".

Captain Semenyuk's odyssey

I had first met Captain Semenyuk, from the Donbas, in 2014 when he was taking part in a skirmish for Donetsk airport. Then a year later at Debaltseve as he was lying on a stretcher - one of the hundreds injured alongside the 270 Ukrainian soldiers killed in a battle during which the separatists, backed by Russian artillery, had the whip hand.

I met him again in the city of Lisichansk, in the Donbas, this May. It was here in the east that the separatist war in Donetsk and Luhansk which led to the dismemberment of Ukraine eight years ago had taken place. And it was here that the Russian forces were now focusing.

The war in Donbas, a hard land of coal mines and steel plants, is vicious and personal. Many on the opposing sides come from the same communities, even the same family at times. Some used to serve together in the police and the military before in what are now the pro-Russian enclaves.

When Leonid Gubarov died fighting the separatists, posthumously receiving a "Hero of Ukraine" award, his father was fighting for the other side. Anton Diachenko, a gunner in Lysychansk, spoke of the half-brother he grew up with now serving in the forces of the Donetsk "People's Republic". Bogdan, a marine, told me of his attempts to reach his mother and 15-year-old sister who are trapped in a separatist area of Luhansk.

The message from the Ukrainian forces were that they were getting out-gunned, not having enough long-range guns or rockets to respond to ferocious Russian artillery assaults, and were low on ammunition. Promised advanced western weaponry simply was not coming through anything like fast enough to make a difference.

Bogdan, the marine, injured, wincing with pain from the shrapnel in his back, said while awaiting treatment: "The shelling is brutal, they focus on a target and they just keep pouring in round after round, we are losing a lot. Unless we get weapons to counter the Russians, get a fighting chance, then I think a lot of us have to face the possibility of getting killed."

Captain Semenyuk said, "It's very tough now. We need to hang on and hope the new weapons will arrive. This is going to be a very long war, I am sure we'll win at the end, but how many of us will be here to see that? I don't know."

About the contributor

Kim Sengupta is the World Affairs Editor of *The Independent*. He has reported on international affairs from a vast number of counties over many years and covered more than two dozen wars. He has won a number of awards for his work.

Away from the 'bang-bang'

Not all war reporting is about war. Richard Pendlebury of the *Daily Mail* carved out a niche in the early days of the war with pieces away from the fighting. The offbeat. Here, in a special dispatch for this book, he recalls two telling vignettes

In a cottage garden under a cerulean sky, a spring afternoon is disturbed only by the crowing of a cockerel and the bark of a distant dog. A breeze rustles through the cherry trees. But otherwise silence prevails. By this point in the war, a wholly unaccustomed silence.

For almost two months we had witnessed and reported on Putin's brutal assault on northern Ukraine. Our north west horizon was marked by smoke from a perpetual fuel fire in the frontline district of Hostomel. A missile blast shattered our sleep and the Little Opera house in downtown Kyiv. And, from the 23rd floor of a shuddering tower block on another hellish night, we looked down upon the never to be forgotten vista of an artillery barrage hitting Irpin.

Thwarted around Ukraine's capital, the Russians withdrew. But a new and more disturbing phase of reporting began: the revealed evidence of mass murder in Bucha, Motyzhyn and other communities where homes, gardens, forests are still giving up their innocent dead.

Photographer Jamie Wiseman and I were among the first journalists to come upon the ghastly half kilometre of civilian corpses and cars, strewn along the E40 highway, west of Kyiv. This revelation took place on an April afternoon of cloying mist from which emerged, scene by disgusting scene, the purple, orange and blackened bodies, stuck by fatty deposit to the shrapnel covered tarmac near pitted roadside signs indicating toilet and cafe stops of the kind you might see on the A303. A modern Gothic horror. Then a Ukrainian armoured column surged across our path, leaving in its wake an ambushed Russian counterpart and further, but more recently cooked, human remains.

'Hard to read,' said one reader comment underneath one of our online reports.

Hard to report, we felt, increasingly.

You cannot do this every day, forever. There has to be light as well as shade. You must remove yourself, if you can, from the grind of the meat grind or go mad. Or numb, and bore the removed reader, who feels they have heard it all before, yesterday.

Vignette one: The untouched dacha

There were brief, unexpected, interludes in this war, informed by beauty and hope rather than hate and destruction. We sought them, for what they were worth.

Some happened by chance. In early March we were interviewing those sheltering in a Kyiv Metro station when we came across Oleksandr, his wife Liza and two daughters, Arina, 13, and Polina, 6. They were huddled miserably on one of the platforms, waiting for a train that would take mother and children to the west of Ukraine and out of the immediate firing line. It was the day before Liza's birthday. There would be no celebration.

The next day our then fixer's resolve broke in the face of expected Russian victory. She too fled to western Ukraine. Oleksandr was waiting for his call up to the over-subscribed territorial defence units. Until that time, he agreed to become our new translator.

And that is how we met his parents, Anatolii and Nadia. Both were retired engineers and, as I wrote then, 'until the war came had hardly spent a day of their 53 years together, apart.'

They invited us to their tiny flat on the 10th floor of a crumbling Soviet era block in Obolon, to eat Nadia's homemade *deruny*– potato pancakes - pickled cucumber and a hot sauce called *adjika*.

The ingredients for these traditional delicacies had been grown in the garden of the family's *dacha*- country cottage - on the edge of a village more than an hour's drive west of the city.

Anatolii and Nadi were worried about their *dacha*. Russian armour had reached the village, they had been told. The whole area was part of a contested frontline. And it was almost planting season. If they could not plant, Nadia could not make *deruny* and pickled cucumbers. Those dishes made with ingredients bought from a supermarket would not be the same.

And so, with the retreat of the Russians from Kyiv, we set out to find if their house was still standing. Not the main news story of the day, but important to us and to them.

Buds showed on every roadside hedgerow and tree; huge fields lay beyond. I wondered what these vistas would look like in the full bloom of May. Or indeed in high summer, just before harvest. The Ukrainian national flag depicts such a scene: a field of corn under a deep blue sky.

And there was the rub. Ukraine is the bread-basket of Europe, the fifth largest exporter of wheat in the world. Much of the grain from the last harvest remained in silos, workers had gone to fight, the Russians had seized agricultural territory. Anatolii and Nadia's concern about their potatoes for *deruny* was a microscopic version of a national and international problem caused by Putin's attack.

Their fears grew as we reached the neighbouring settlement of Byshiv. A row of cottages had been destroyed. So, the war *had* come to their district. We'd seen it all before but it was no less shocking on that glorious spring day.

But all was well, in fact. The gates of their dacha were un-breached. Anatoli fumbled with the padlock. Beside the entrance a Tartarian honeysuckle was in bud.

The little dacha - only three small rooms of wood and clay and half a hectare of land - has been in Nadia's family for a century. Windows had been broken by blast in three neighbouring farms. Theirs was untouched by the conflict.

The garden was exquisite. Bees buzzed among the Siberian squill, white hyacinths and purple 'glory of the snow', all in full bloom. A painted lady butterfly flitted about the orchard of cherry, plum, apricot, walnut and apple trees. Somewhere a skylark was singing. This was pure Tolstoy.

Nadia began to clear away the dried brush that had been placed over the garlic and strawberry beds against the winter frost.

A neighbour who owned a tractor would come and turn the soil. And then the couple would plant cabbage, potatoes, carrots, corn, cucumbers and salad. In May they would move into the *dacha* and remain there until October, as always.

'If it is still safe,' qualified Nadia, wistfully.

We left them there, feeling a little better about the prospects for humanity, as we did one afternoon earlier in the war.

Vignette Two: Bulgakov in the basement

We were in the back room of a basement restaurant on Andreevsky Prospect.

Outside Kyiv was closed, barricaded and under attack. But in here a woman was giving a talk - in Russian - about the great Kyivan writer Mikhail Bulgakov. And the room was packed with locals who had chosen to stay, under siege, rather than become refugees. With the barbarians at the gates, the event was an act of cultural defiance.

Bulgakov was born and studied in Kyiv. His family home, now a museum, is further down Andreevsky Prospect. His most acclaimed work - one of the greatest novels of the 20thCentury - is the dark satire *The Master and Margarita*.

The plot is pertinent to the current time and situation, concerning the visit of Satan to Soviet-era Moscow.

In recent years Bulgakov has become the subject of a cultural tug of war between Ukraine and Russia. Though resident in Kyiv his middle-class family spoke Russian at home. Bulgakov wrote in Russian and moved to Moscow when he was in his twenties.

Russian nationalists have claimed him as their own. Last year (2021) Ukraine's President Zelenskyy - who himself grew up speaking Russian as a first language - felt moved to issue a statement to say that Russian language versions of *The Master and Margarita* had not been banned from being imported into his country.

I spoke to Lyudmyla Gubianuri, the director of the Mikhail Bulgakov Museum.

'Which country does Bulgakov belong to, Russia or Ukraine?' she asked. 'To both, just like Gogol, Tchaikovsky and Prokofiev. This war is our pain'.' I don`t know how Bulgakov himself would comment on it but as a doctor he definitely hated wars'. He wrote: "All the wars be damned forever and ever".

Back to 'bang-bang'

But you cannot escape Putin's war. It was waiting for us only a few miles beyond Anatoli and Nadia's dacha.

In the forest on either side of the road, slender pines have been felled by tank fire. A footbridge has been brought down, across the western carriageway of the E40. At a ruined petrol station next to the empty village of Buzovaya two Russian T-72 tanks were charred wrecks.

These losses seem to have spurred the tank unit into a frenzy of revenge. Certainly, the signs were of a military formation that had lost all discipline.

Like many petrol stations this one has been comprehensively looted by the invader. The gutters ran with alcohol. On one wall a Russian has sprayed in English, 'Bad Company 13' and on another, in Russian, 'Ukrainians you will be fucking dead!'

The threat was carried out. A blood smeared storm drain behind the petrol station was used for the disposal of at least two corpses.

So much for bucolic interludes.

Yet there was much to be thankful for. Having been granted refugee visas, Oleks' family have now reached London and safety. He was 'relieved' though he still could not sleep properly for Bucha nightmares. Nor can I. The Russian forces are pushing anew, on the Eastern front. The Devil remains in Moscow. The little pleasures of 'normal' life are still elusive in Ukraine.

About the contributor

Richard Pendlebury is a staff writer at the *Daily Mail*. He covered his first war in the former Yugoslavia and since then has reported from conflicts in Chechnya, Iraq, Afghanistan, North Africa and across the Middle East.

On the ground in Kyiv … newspapers and the war

The Russian invasion of Ukraine is a story so big that it initially knocked Covid, Partygate and everything else off the front pages. Former *Times* night editor turned media commentator Liz Gerard looks at the editorial choices newspapers are having to make when covering the conflict

On 9 April 2003, American tanks rolled into Baghdad. Saddam Hussein was in hiding and an emboldened crowd tied a rope around his statue, pulled it down, then started beating it with slippers - which we soon learnt was the greatest insult an Iraqi can deliver.

Sitting on a Fleet Street backbench, the choice of picture for the next day's paper was relatively easy. There were three candidates: the statue as it was being pulled down, an American soldier putting a US flag on Saddam's head, or - the one we went with at *The Times* - a US Marine looking over his shoulder at the statue, by then at 90° to its plinth.

For the tabloids, the headline was easy too: the *Sun* and *Mirror* went with 'Statue of Liberty', the *Mail* and *Express* a single word: 'Toppled'. Both the *Guardian* and *Telegraph* took a similar approach, with 'The toppling of Saddam'. But we at The *Times* just had to be different. Heaven knows why we couldn't have gone with the obvious. I remember the duty editor sitting at my side, agonising over a form of words that would capture the historic nature of the day. We ended up with 'Victory in the 21-day war'. Well, that aged well, didn't it?

I didn't like it then - and not because of any prescience that our troops would be in Iraq for years - and I still cringe to think of it now. I daresay its author is none too proud of it either. The point of this anecdote is not to reopen old wounds, but to point up one of the pitfalls of covering a war: latching on to a single dramatic event and over-egging it to imbue it with a significance that may not be borne out in retrospect.

This is true of all journalism to some extent; we are very fortunate if we recognise a turning point at the moment it happens. We may think we've spotted one and say, "things will never be the same again" and then they revert to normal - and then we go and miss the removal of the single domino that brings a whole edifice crashing down.

War is thankfully so alien to us that the dangers of misinterpretation are magnified - just when there is the greatest duty to get it as right as possible. So how do we go about that? Like the armies who are doing the real fighting: by marshalling our forces to maximise our strengths and calling in reinforcements to limit our weaknesses.

The role of the foreign editor

The war correspondent is the legendary journalistic hero - even down to poor old Boot in *Scoop*. He or - more frequently these days - she is the one putting themselves in danger. But it is foreign editors, directing operations from the office, who carry the heaviest load. They not only have to make sure that people in the field have the right equipment and documentation and that they are in the right place, but they have to be super-mindful of their correspondents' physical safety and mental health, to pick up signals that they might be putting themselves at too much risk or under too much strain.

They also have to oversee the overall coverage - first-person stuff from on the spot is what everyone wants to read, but we also need an oversight of the entire conflict and the geopolitics. And that comes from the office - from the political team, the defence editor, the diplomatic editor, as well as foreign correspondents in the key capitals and at the UN. We also need expert analysis and interpretation, so reliable voices from outside the office have to be found.

New *Times*: Lack of resources

At the time of the Iraq war, the *Times* had at least ten staffers in the Gulf, as well as all those people in London. It has just two in Ukraine - plus the bonus of the veteran war photographer Jack Hill, a luxury few others enjoy. Former foreign editor Martin Fletcher says: "They probably sent more people to China in advance of the 2008 Olympics." The one improvement on those days, Fletcher adds, is that communications are much better now.

This depletion of resources is the same for everyone. All newspaper staffing has been cut to the bone over the past 20 years, so that there is a huge reliance on stringers - both in the warzone and in the offices at home and abroad. What's more, the workload has increased, with not only a print deadline to meet, but the constant demand to feed the online beast, not to mention tweets, podcasts, videos.

A partial picture

There are two million refugees in Poland, but who is there to tell that story? And there is, of course, no reliable source of information on what is happening in Russia. The news editor Marina Ovsyannikova's public dissent made every front page and we know that she was arrested and fined 30,000 roubles. We saw her as a heroine, we feared for her safety and wondered how she could stay in the country. But we had absolutely no way of knowing how many Russians saw her protest or what impact it made in her home country.

There has been speculation about Putin's health and his and foreign minister Sergey Lavrov's pronouncements have been analysed to within an inch of their lives. But random interviews with people on the street brave enough to express a counter view cannot be taken as representative of what the nation thinks, so there has been a huge black hole where the true Russian perspective should be.

Even with such constraints and the diminished workforce, the war (or any huge running story - Covid was the same) generates far more copy than could ever be accommodated in print. The web may have infinite space, but you still need the subs to process and upload the material - and their numbers have been cut even more ruthlessly than those of any other department.

Finding the right balance

And that's where the next pitfall lies: in balancing your product. War is good for business, bringing in sales and increased audiences as people who might not generally care much about world affairs come into the fold. You have lots to say about the war, but you also want to cater for those with gloom fatigue - which is most people after six years of Brexit and pandemic - and, from a commercial imperative, showcase all the other wonderful things you do to encourage your new audience to stick with you.

For the first two weeks after the invasion, most papers allowed their Ukraine coverage to run straight through from the front, with only the *Telegraph* offering different fare on pages 2 and 3 from the word go. Gradually, all titles pushed the conflict pages back in the book and other subjects appeared on the fronts, while broadcasters, with the advantage of live footage, stuck with Ukraine.

On the day P&O sacked 800 workers by Zoom and Nazanin Zaghari-Radcliffe came home, *BBC News* had film from Kharkiv, Mariupol and Odesa, plus a political assessment from John Simpson before reporting on the domestic news. There was room for only three stories - the ferries, Nazanin and inflation - before it was back to Ukraine.

This was far from a fair reflection of the day's events at home and abroad - even Covid, with numbers of infections soaring on the eve of the lifting of all travel restrictions, didn't get a mention. But time isn't elastic and when you've invested licence-fee payers' money in sending reporters and camera crews to Ukraine, you want to air every offering.

Missing other stories

Newspapers are in a better position on this - paradoxically, partly because the staffing cuts mean there are slightly fewer conflict reports competing for space than during the Iraq and Afghanistan wars. They still have room for other material. But what other material? When you have three or four war spreads and possibly another on the coronavirus, you need something to leaven the mix. And so you end up with a surfeit of war reports followed by a disproportionate amount of fluff, leaving the reader bloated but unsatisfied from too much stodge, too much pud and too few green vegetables. By that, I mean the good-for-you (as opposed to feelgood) stories on serious issues; matters of policy and society.

This is wonderful for politicians who want to escape scrutiny, brushing aside challenges on almost any topic with today's equivalent of "Don't you know there's a war on?" But it's not good for democracy.

Important legislation has been working its way through parliament this Spring, bills that affect people's right to live here, to protest, to use the internet. The government has suffered setbacks in some aspects of its legislative programme and has made progress in others, yet all of this has gone largely unreported by mainstream news outlets. If you want to know how the Lords voted on the Nationalities Bill, *Twitter* will offer you more information than the *Telegraph*.

This stuff is important and it is being lost under cover of war, virtue-signalling refugee appeals and pictures of the Duchess of Cambridge.

Adrenalin rush

And as to all that war reporting - all those UN meetings, phone calls between leaders, even the human-interest stories - how much is actually being read? I've been here, through the decline of the Soviet empire, the fall of the Berlin Wall, the Gulf War, the Balkans, Iraq, Afghanistan, Chechnya, the "colour" revolutions. When you're putting a paper together, these stories are intoxicating. They dominate your life and you can't get enough of them (I was absolutely hooked on *BBC Gulf FM*), so you assume the reader shares your obsession. Most don't. However brilliant the writing.

For those who do, there has been some excellent reporting out of Ukraine, on screen and in print. *Channel 4 News'* Lindsey Hilsum is fantastic as is Alex Thomson; Thomas Friedman of the *New York Times* and Lawrence Freedman in the *New Statesman* are worth your time. Anthony Loyd in the *Times* is probably the best war correspondent working today and Henry Foy in the FT is another must-read. Security expert Fiona Hill pops up all over the place - from *Politico* to *the Economist* and *the Scotsman* - and knows what she's talking about. The list goes on and on.

So, if you want to know about the Ukraine war, go for the heavyweights; if you want to know about kind-hearted Brits and royals, go for the tabloids; if you want to know about day-to-day policy developments, sadly, your best bet is social media.

And never forget that when war breaks out, no matter how hard reporters strive to bring us the truth - and, by golly, they do - everything you see or hear is what someone on one side or the other wants you to see or hear. Keep your wits about you and good luck!

This piece first appeared in *Inpublishing* in April 2022.

About the contributor

Liz Gerard worked for *The Times* for more than 30 years, latterly as night editor and business night editor. She now writes about print journalism for, inter alia, *Inpublishing, Press Gazette* and the *New European*. She was named media commentator of the year at the EI Comment Awards in 2014 and 2016.

WAR CONVENTIONAL AND NOT

***

Belling the cat. Metadata and manipulation: the build up to and invasion of Ukraine

In the run-up to the invasion of Ukraine, the Russian Government and its allies twisted and fabricated events to justify it. But the online community, including Bellingcat, who use online information to investigate events, was ready for it, writes Nick Waters

The Russian Government has a rather peculiar/interesting relationship with reality. While Western Governments often play fast and loose with facts, it is sometimes difficult to understand quite how absurd the Russian Government's relationship with the truth has become. For example, when the Russian Ministry of Defence (MoD) published easily disprovable faked satellite images in an attempt to blame Ukraine for the shooting down of Malaysian Airlines Flight MH 17[1], or when state-run Channel One broadcast footage from the computer game Arma-3 on the premise that it showed combat in Syria[2]. Or when Mr Putin himself was caught showing footage of American troops in Afghanistan claiming it was Russians fighting ISIS[3]. Or when the Russian MoD claimed it had "irrefutable evidence" of US troops aiding the Islamic State, which turned out to be footage from the computer game "AC-130 Gunship Simulator"[4]. As you might see, there's a bit of a theme here.

Disinformation as a way of life

These aren't only simple mistakes on the part of the Russian institutions. Deliberate disinformation by the Russian state is used alongside its military power to achieve strategic objectives. During the first invasion of Ukraine in 2014, Mr Putin claimed, despite the absolutely overwhelming evidence to the contrary, that Russian troops were not involved[5]. Although even at the time this statement was clearly absurd, it had the effect of sowing doubt and division within the world community about how best to respond to Russia's invasion.

A more focused example is the disinformation campaign that targeted the Syrian Civil Defence (SCD), often referred to as the White Helmets. A Western-funded search and rescue organisation based in rebel-held Syria, they came to prominence for pulling people out of the rubble from Syrian regime and Russian airstrikes. Due to their policy of wearing helmet cameras they also became one of the most prominent sources of information regarding the brutal campaign that Bashar al Assad was waging against his own people. The result was a massive (dis?) information campaign which painted the SCD as 'terrorists', including blaming them for the chemical attacks carried out by the Syrian regime. This campaign had a significant amount of success, undermining the information provided by the SCD, making it more difficult for them to gather funding and ultimately painted these rescue workers as 'legitimate targets'[6] who could be targeted and killed like any other combatant.

Before the February Invasion

So, when Russia built up its forces in Ukraine in early 2022, while at the same time claiming that they had no intention of invading, we were a bit sceptical.

At Bellingcat, we are intimately familiar with the approach that the Russian Government takes to these kinds of events. We strongly suspected that an information campaign would precede the actual launch of hostilities. Sure enough, in the run up to the invasion the Russian state attempted to generate a narrative that the 'Neo-Nazi' Ukrainians were staging a huge build-up in the Donbass with the intent of invading separatist-held areas. As part of this narrative, the 'Neo-Nazi' 'Ukrainians would, of course, create provocations in order to generate a pretext to invade.

What we saw over the first weeks of February 2022 was the Russian Government's attempt to support this narrative. Luckily for us, attempts to fake attacks and provocations by the Ukrainian Government were amateurish and transparently false. It helped that a community of analysts, journalists and hobbyists, formed on the internet and forged through multiple conflicts, was already waiting in the wings, ready to pore over every scrap of information that the Russian Government released.

Verification or not?

This was done using processes of verification that had developed over the previous decade to assess the validity of information emerging online from confusing situations, primarily conflict zones. Each image or video tells a story, and sometimes that story is different from the claim which accompanies it. For example, a person could post a video of a protest in the Middle East claiming it is in Iran, but on closer inspection some people in the crowd are carrying Iraqi flags and the street signs are in Arabic, rather than Persian. This is probably quite a strong indicator that the video is actually in Iraq and the poster is, in fact, a bad liar.

By placing the video exactly in space, a process known as geolocation, it may be possible to establish precisely when the video was filmed and thereby even identify the precise event during which the video was filmed.

Sometimes the tell-tale information isn't the image or video itself, but rather it's metadata: data embedded in the image or video by the device which recorded it. Metadata records a multitude of factors, including the time it was taken and sometimes even the GPS coordinates. Most social media platforms delete this metadata, but Telegram, which is incredibly popular in Russia and Ukraine, sometimes does not.

The computer says 'no'

On 18 February the leaders of the self-proclaimed Donetsk and Luhansk People's Republics (DPR & LPR) announced an evacuation of their civilians into Russia, claiming the recent escalation in fighting due to apparent Ukrainian aggression was a threat to them. These statements were filmed and published on the official *Telegram* channels, leaving the metadata intact. Sharp eyed observers noticed that the metadata of these videos showed they had been filmed on the 16 February 2022, two days before the official pronouncements and while the "escalation" was still in its early days.

Also on the 18 February, a video[7] was released by the DPR which claimed to show bodycam footage from a group of Polish speaking men who had apparently attacked a sewage facility in separatist-held Horlivka, attempting to blow up a canister of chlorine gas. Needless to say, this attack was heroically thwarted. The incident immediately came under suspicion due to the central role that Russian disinformation has played in relation to chemical weapons attacks in Syria, often blaming first responders and victims themselves for carrying out attacks which had been perpetrated by the Syrian regime[8].

Once again, the metadata associated with the video demonstrated that this apparent chemical attack was completely fabricated. It showed that the video had been filmed on the 8 February, well before the attack had reportedly taken place. Even more damning, it was discovered that the sound of explosions heard within the video had been edited in, and had been taken from a video depicting a Finnish military exercise[9].!

'Bodies and bones'?

The most egregious example of these fabricated incidents took place on 22 February, when an IED (Improvised Explosive Device), reportedly placed by the Ukrainian army, allegedly killed three civilians. Grisly footage taken by journalists and activists showed the aftermath, with three burnt bodies shown in gruesome detail in the back of a civilian vehicle.

Once again, eagle eyed members of the online community noticed discrepancies with this account, with the most suspicious feature being a series of straight cuts to the skull of one of the victims. These cuts looked less like damage caused by an IED, and much more like a surgical procedure carried out during an autopsy. We investigated this incident further, asking the opinions of an explosive weapons expert and forensic pathologists, all of whom concluded that the details seen regarding this incident were not consistent with an IED, but were consistent with the victims having undergone autopsy before their bodies were burnt in the car.[10]

Most gallingly, the Russian Government has repeatedly accused the Syrian opposition of faking chemical weapons attacks using bodies taken from morgues, not only without evidence, but often in the face of extremely good evidence demonstrating the Syrian regime was responsible[11]. Yet this is precisely what Russian-back separatists, who are under the influence of the Russian Government, appear to have done in this case in Ukraine.

Good information is out there

It is easy to draw the conclusion from these events that nothing on the internet can be trusted, yet this would not only be wrong, it also plays into the hands of those, like the Russian Government, who actively want to make people doubt that objective truth can ever be found. Or, in the words of Peter Pomerantsev, that "nothing is true and everything is possible".[12]

The reality is that the vast majority of content seen online regarding conflict is legitimate information which can be captured, preserved and most importantly, verified. Once this process is complete it can be used either for journalistic endeavours or even as evidence for accountability purposes.

Ultimately, Bellingcat's goal in the days before 24 February was to examine and, if necessary, debunk narratives pushed by the Russian Government which were used to justify the invasion. Despite this justification falling flat, Russia invaded on the 24 February 2022 and started a new war which has, so far, cost the lives of tens of thousands of people. However, unlike in Syria, where Russia had some success in painting all parts of civil society as jihadists, its 'Neo Nazi' narrative justifying the war in Ukraine was relatively unsuccessful, at least in Europe and North America.

Post invasion

With the invasion, Bellingcat's focus has switched to accountability, both for journalistic and legal purposes. We are recording examples of civilian harm in Ukraine as a result of the conflict, taking care not to differentiate that caused by Russia or Ukraine. While we recognise that international justice is a long road, we hope that by demonstrating clearly that we are watching, we may mitigate at least some of the horrors of war, and maybe eventually help to bring perpetrators to justice.

Notes

[1] Higgins, Eliot (2015) 'New July 17th Satellite Imagery Confirms Russia Produced Fake MH17 Evidence', *Bellingcat,* 15 June. Available at https://www.bellingcat.com/news/uk-and-europe/2015/06/12/july-17-imagery-mod-comparison/ (Accessed: 25 April 2022)

[2] BBC Monitoring (2018) 'Russian TV airs video game as Syria war footage', BBC, 26 February. Available at https://www.bbc.co.uk/news/blogs-news-from-elsewhere-43198324 (Accessed: 25 April 2022)

[3] Novak, Matt (2017) 'Video That Putin Shows Oliver Stone of Russians Fighting ISIS is Totally Fake [Updated]', *Gizmodo,* 20 June. Available at: https://gizmodo.com/video-that-putin-shows-oliver-stone-of-russians-fightin-1796257586 (Accessed: 25 April 2022)

[4] Higgins, Eliot (2017) 'The Russian Ministry of Defence Publishes Screenshots of Computer Games as Evidence of US Collusion with ISIS', *Bellingcat,* 14 November. Available at: https://www.bellingcat.com/news/mena/2017/11/14/russian-ministry-defence-publishes-screenshots-computer-games-evidence-us-collusion-isis/ (Accessed: 25 April 2022)

[5] Chappell, Bill & Memmott, Mark (2014) 'Putin Says Those Aren't Russian Forces In Crimea', *NPR,* 4 March. Available at https://www.npr.org/sections/thetwo-way/2014/03/04/285653335/putin-says-those-arent-russian-forces-in-crimea (Accessed: 15 May 2022)

[6] Loveluck, Louisa (2018) 'Russian disinformation campaign targets Syria's beleaguered rescue workers', *The Washington Post,* 18 December, Available at: https://www.washingtonpost.com/world/russian-disinformation-campaign-targets-syrias-beleaguered-rescue-workers/2018/12/18/113b03c4-02a9-11e9-8186-4ec26a485713_story.html (Accessed: 15 May 2022)

[7] People's Militia of the DPR, [@nm_dnr] (2022) Video [Telegram] 18 February. Available at:

[8] Bellingcat Investigation Team (2018) 'Chemical Weapons and Absurdity: The Disinformation Campaign Against the White Helmets', *Bellingcat,* 18 December, Available at: https://www.bellingcat.com/news/mena/2018/12/18/chemical-weapons-and-absurdity-the-disinformation-campaign-against-the-white-helmets/ (Accessed: 17 May 2022)

[9] Higgins, Eliot, [@eliothiggins] (2022) 'Anatomy of a Russian Separatist False Flag', [Twitter] 20 February. Available at: https://twitter.com/EliotHiggins/status/1495355366141534208 (Accessed: 17 May 2022)

[10] Waters, Nick (2022) "Exploiting Cadavers 'and 'Faked IEDs': Experts Debunk Staged Pre-War 'Provocation' in the Donbas', *Bellingcat,* 28 February, Available at: https://www.bellingcat.com/news/2022/02/28/exploiting-cadavers-and-faked-ieds-experts-debunk-staged-pre-war-provocation-in-the-donbas/ (Accessed: 17 May 2022)

[11] Grigoriev, Maxim (2020) 'Remarks by Mr. Maxim Grigoriev, Head of the Foundation for the Study of Democracy, at an Arria-formula meeting of UNSC member states', *Permanent Mission of the Russian Federation to the United Nations,* 20 January, Available at: https://russiaun.ru/en/news/opcwngo200120 (Accessed: 17 May 2022)

[12] Pomerantsev, Peter (2014) *Nothing is True and Everything Is Possible*, New York: Public Affairs

About the contributor

Nick Waters is a senior investigator at Bellingcat, where he's worked since 2018. With a background as a British Army infantry officer, Nick has always been interested in the application of open source investigation to conflict, writing about chemical weapons in Syria, airstrikes in Yemen and the use of small drones by sub-state actors. His current focus is on the use of open source information as evidence for accountability purposes.

Aerorozvidka. Civilian drone operators bring lethal asymmetric capabilities to the frontline

The Aerorozvidka group was founded in 2014 by civilians wanting to deploy their drone skills against the Russian incursion into Ukraine. In the 2022 war they are on the frontlines, providing countrywide reconnaissance and the delivery of lethal force against Russian assets. Dr Dominic Selwood writes about the drone war

There are not many crowd-funded tech start-ups with the punching power to halt a 40-mile convoy of military heavy armour. Yet, while the world watched Russia's horrifying advance on Kyiv in March 2002, that is exactly what happened. Working with units of the Ukrainian military, a group of civilians rigged up drones with thermal imaging cameras and high explosives, waited until nightfall, then bombed the vehicles leading the Russian convoy, creating an obstacle of mangled metal that nothing could manoeuvre past on the narrow, forest-lined road. Stranded, the column eventually dispersed, abandoning any assault on Kyiv. 'We are patriots', explained Mykhaylo, a senior member of the group, speaking to me on a secure connection from an undisclosed location in Ukraine, 'defending our country against the enemy. I can say with honour that we helped stop them reaching Kyiv'.

Civilian irregulars

The organisation's name is Aerorozvidka, or 'aerial reconnaissance'. It was founded as a group of irregulars at the start of the Russian invasion in 2014 by Volodymyr Kochetkov-Sukac, a former investment banker nicknamed 'Chewbacca'. He was killed in Donbas in 2015 retrieving a drone downed behind enemy lines, but his organisation is very much alive, and is now a key player in the country's defence.

Aerorozvidka is a non-military organisation of 'technically aware citizens', who pool their skills in order to fight. They are a tight-knit group, with dozens currently active in the ranks, and number well over a hundred including reservists. The teams comprise men and women, ranging from teenagers to seniors - one is known as 'Grandpa' - and include students, PhDs, teachers, scientists, drone hobbyists, and business people. Their size has swelled appreciably since the February invasion, with members of the military now also joining in strength, bringing a wide palette of combat expertise to operations. Being such a diverse group, its members come from a wide range of backgrounds across Ukraine. Once largely Kyiv-centred, the organisation now has branches all around the country.

Command structure

Aerorozvidka operates in three divisions: reconnaissance, fighting, and cybersecurity.

The reconnaissance and cybersecurity sections have been building a situation-awareness system since 2014. Known as DELTA, it aggregates information from reconnaissance drones, satellites and human intelligence sources to create a multi-layered map of enemy military activity. It was tested during a recent 'Sea Breeze' Nato-Ukrainian exercise in the Black Sea, and proved itself fully Nato standard. As the internet in Ukraine is compromised, Aerorozvidka passes the intelligence gathered by DELTA via Elon Musk's Starlink satellite system to all elements of the Ukrainian military establishment, and it has proved invaluable in accurately pinpointing Russian military assets, including for targeting by heavy artillery.

The fighting section is centred around weaponised drones. In 2014 the group began operations with off-the-shelf commercial drones like the Chinese DJI Phantom, but now it largely designs and builds its own from scratch. These can be composite drones assembled from a wide range of different parts and models, although their trademark unit is the R18: a formidable-looking octocopter with a 1.5-metre span capable of carrying and releasing five-kilogram explosive devices.

Aerorozvidka's drone units are deployed for both strikes and reconnaissance. The fighting section works with all parts of the Ukrainian military, to which it also provides training and full-service drone customisation and maintenance. Its operatives have been in the field since the start of the invasion, seeing action on day one against Russian paratroopers landing at Hostomel Airport to the north-west of Kyiv.

The third section, cybersecurity, is no less busy than the other two, as DELTA receives multiple cyberattacks every day. These are typically from disguised Russian IP addresses bounced through multiple countries but, on one occasion recently, the attacker failed to mask its IP address, which duly disclosed a location inside the Kremlin.

Funding

Aerorozvidka is technically a non-governmental organisation: effectively a not-for-profit charity. It receives no financial support from the Ukrainian government, but relies entirely on cash donations via its website and active social media accounts. 'We are hugely grateful to all people and all organisations that support us', Mykhaylo, who is a board member, is keen to say. 'We receive hundreds of messages with support and warm words, and people all over the world send us everything from a few Euro to thousands of dollars'. The group also receives donations of drones, equipment, and parts from across the globe, whether brand new or old units gathering dust in garages.

The financial spend-to-reward ratio of operations is compelling. Drones costing several dozen thousand dollars to assemble, kit-out and deploy regularly destroy high-value vehicles like T-72 battle tanks, rocket launchers, fuel trucks, and others whose individual costs can stretch into the millions of dollars. Drones can be reused infinite times, unless destroyed, and their ability to inflict such crippling, disproportionate damage makes them highly financially effective, marking a significant evolution in the economics of modern warfare.

Like any organisation in the process of scaling up, central purchasing from manufacturers is now the priority, as the teams require solid supplies of drones, thermal imaging cameras, and a range of other specialist equipment, some of which is dual-purpose and subject to restrictive export controls. 'If a relevant manufacturer wants us to test their equipment', Mykhaylo offers in all seriousness, 'please send it to us, and we will give you detailed feedback on performance in the battlefield'. Aerorozvidka is, though, he is quick to add, a not-for-profit organisation of patriots fighting an existential war of attrition to defend their country. They are not a commercial venture, and have no equipment or technology for sale. Their sole remit is to support Ukrainian military defence activity.

Democratising warfare

Across the globe, the wars of recent years have increasingly been asymmetrical, pitting forces of strikingly differing strengths and tactics against one another. The role, importance and impact that a small but highly skilled civilian organisation of irregulars like Aerorozvidka can have against a country like Russia with a total military and paramilitary force of over 3.5 million people is yet another indication that warfare has morphed forever. Aerorozvidka is proof of the democratisation of today's military conflicts - especially in the increasingly decisive domains of technology and cyber - such that every citizen can be an effective combatant. As Mykhaylo notes of their reconnaissance and pinpoint drone attacks that were so decisive in defeating 40 miles of traditional military hard power around Kvij, 'This is the modern way to do these operations. The Russians simply didn't expect it'.

A version of this article first appeared in *The New Statesman* on 12 May 2022.

About the contributor

Dr Dominic Selwood is a historian, broadcaster, journalist and barrister. He is a bestselling author and novelist, and frequent contributor to national newspapers, radio and TV including the *Telegraph*, the *Independent*, the *New Statesman*, the *Spectator*, the BBC and Sky. He has a doctorate in history from Oxford University and a masters from the Sorbonne, and served as a Captain in the British Army reserve. He is a Fellow of the Royal Historical Society and the Society of Antiquaries.

Adversarial networks: the first AI War

Ukraine is a battle of artillery and information. Paradigms have shifted for how participants - from soldiers to countries - collect and deploy facts. Natural language processing, computer vision and deep learning are powerful new weapons. Ukraine is the first AI war, argues Dr Alex Connock

Move 37 was a watershed moment in popular conception of Artificial Intelligence - the apparently trivial placement of a piece in the ancient Chinese strategy game, Go. The move was made by an AI agent named AlphaGo, playing then world champion, Lee Sedol, in Seoul, South Korea in 2016, after he had stepped outside for a cigarette break.

Alpha Go was created by the Google-owned computer science company DeepMind, one of a sequence of increasingly expert and autonomous systems. One system taught itself to play chess in a single day, unassisted by humans; by tea-time, having played tens of thousands of games against itself, it could beat any player in the history of the world.

His smoking break over, Lee Sedol came back to the Go table, to find the AI had done something strange - putting a piece on the opposite side to the game action. Experts dismissed this move as irrelevant. No human player would have even considered it.

Some 100 moves later, Alpha Go won the game. Move 37 had restructured the strategic play, the pivotal piece that defined the significance of every move before and after. World champion Sedol said: "I thought AlphaGo was based on probability calculation, and that it was merely a machine. But when I saw this move I changed my mind. Surely AlphaGo is creative." Lots of experts don't think AI is creative - but few disagree that it has *zeitgeist*-re-defining, calculating power. The boss of DeepMind, Demis Hassabis, said: "Whatever the question, the answer is AI."

The Ukraine War and Move 37

So what has that got to do with the war in the Ukraine?

The answer is that the Ukraine war has also been a Move 37 moment. Just as the Go gambit changed games, so a similarly profound dynamic is playing out in Ukraine. The first three months of war saw conflict as brutal, manual as much of World War Two. But it saw another kind of war - with and between AI systems - of algorithms, commercial satellites, automated disinformation, and synthetic information, from the *Twitter* bots to full-blown 'deep fakes'. These tools will define not only the outcome of this war, but also the 'gameplay' of shooting wars, and information wars, of the future - just like Move 37.

Sean Gourley, CEO of AI firm Primer, said: "The ability to train and retrain AI models on the fly will become a critical advantage in future wars."[1] Whoever owns the compute power wins.

Let's briefly examine four dimensions of this shift - supervised learning, natural language processing, generative adversarial networks and dynamic content optimisation - and ask how they may signal changes to come in aspects of war, information and journalism.

Supervised Learning

AI is powerful at pattern recognition, detecting nuanced correlations the human might not. Even without an explanatory causal relationship, AI systems can find operationally useful statistical correlation. Owning a horse can predict longevity, not because horses are good for your health - but because being rich is. The length of time it takes to type your name on an online mortgage application predicts your propensity to default on the loan.

Algorithms can be most effective when trained with sample data categorised by humans, called supervised learning. Human guidance teaches a Tesla what a traffic light is, which is why you are endlessly clicking on pictures of traffic lights to access websites.

This is also happening in warfare as AI systems are taught to recognise military assets. As Gregory C. Allen from the Center for Strategic & International Studies wrote: "Even in peacetime, satellites get to take a lot of pictures of Russian and Chinese military forces, and those pictures can be digitally labelled by human experts to turn them into training data. Training data is what machine learning AI systems learn from."

The Z Factor

AI could, for instance, be good for automatically spotting tanks - especially when the Russians helpfully paint a large Z on the side of them.

The Z symbolised three things. For the Russian soldiers - an operational tool to protect from friendly fire. For the Russian nation - a symbolic rallying prompt to be iterated in TV shows and branded goods, which to the rest of the world looked as organically as *Game of Thrones*. And for the opposition it was a potential tool for anyone using aerial or space-based image recognition systems, or the Gray Eagle[2] drones that the US sold to Ukraine in June 2022, to use supervised learning to find tanks and blow them up.

Photos of vehicles with the Z on them provided obvious training data on what a Russian tank looks like. Russian news source *RIA Novosti* itself reported a similar system: "neural network training algorithms, which makes it possible to accurately determine the samples of equipment in a wide variety of environmental conditions, including with a short exposure (the technique is visible for several seconds or less), as well as when only part of the sample falls into the field of view of the drone—when, for example, only part of any combat vehicle is visible from cover."[3]

The Z was a symbolic prompt as potentially valuable as those tangentially-angled shots of fire hydrants and bicycles we all help Captcha[4] categorise. The Z is an example of how Ukraine, with commercial space imagery, has introduced transformative visual transparency into war. It is available to countries at war and commercial operators[5] providing services, in the same way that hedge funds use computer vision to analyse satellite imagery at scale for the number of containers in a port, or the likelihood of a good grain harvest. Analysts observe a change that has taken place in Western intelligence sourcing: "Entirely new realms of data mining, crowd-sourced social media ground intelligence, and commercial earth observation systems that offered satellite imagery rivalling the KEYHOLE national reconnaissance capabilities of an earlier generation."[6]

News outlets, meanwhile, are very slow to adapt the analytical technology at scale, still relying on the 20th century sources of traditional news-gathering by reporters or second-hand information from governments. But it will not be long before major news outlets are using computer vision to produce their own real-time analysis. *The New York Times* is already working on it.[7]

Natural language processing (NLP)

This war is different from any previous engagement because of the quantity of verbal data available - not just the social media firehose (which is enormous - *TikTok* adds 8 users per second[8]) but also un-encrypted military radio traffic. These offer insight into communications and knowledge - if you can translate and categorise the data before everyone moves, which is the critical task for both public and private sector analysis. Capturing language at such vast scale is valuable if you can parse it to actionable insights, and worthless if you cannot. The AI techniques that facilitates that are collectively called NLP.[9]

At least one US commercial firm has ingested most of the publicly-available digital language material in the world - up to 500 billion parameters - and is hungry for more, as each new layer improves the system's ability to predict what comes next in a sequence of words. Such is the volume of data available, that an average of 80 per cent of the average organisation's data remains unstructured. The world's language data is divided into pre-2020 and post-2020 sources, because since 2020, there is a possibility text may have been synthetically created by computer. In a world of bots and fake data, systems can recognise as synthetic text created by all AI tools they know. The risk is that there may be unknown systems.

The organisation that better recognises and deploys synthetic data will win future information wars. The participant that structures this vast lake of content, and which better combines layered information from maps to the social graph will have the most compelling insight. The military which best integrates the data into its 'kinetic' activity will win. Primer.AI collected audio from web feeds emulating radio receiver hardware, transcribing and translating battlefield information - with machine learning that learned Russian slang for military vehicles and weapons.[10] The US Army has a battlefield equivalent called TITAN, which drives around collecting information and analysing it, in which "AI/ML-enabled capabilities and the first Multi-Link/Multi-Band (ML/MB) antenna are considered critical enabling technologies."[11] Accurate data means accurate fire.

Generative Adversarial Networks (GAN)

Much has been made of the creation of a fake video of President Zelenskyy in March 2022. Though it was not a particularly good one[12] - even an amateur could see it was spoofed - it was a sign of things to come. The synthetic video is created using deep learning, so it is called a 'deep fake'. The technique employed is a Generative Adversarial Network.

GANs use two neural networks, each trained on a dataset of verified examples (in this case, presumably, some video of the real President Zelenskyy). A game of cops and robbers is initiated between computer systems. One network, the generator model, creates new imagery which might plausibly have fitted into the original dataset. The other network is the discriminator, which tests the synthetic imagery for its verisimilitude. When the generator model creates synthetic footage that is good enough to trick the discriminator, it has become sufficiently real to be sent out into the world and to trick us.

Fake video is just one weapon in the synthetic content arsenal[13]. This is currently stocked with automated social media influencers - but as the technology develops it will become a powerful and dystopian disinformation tool to justify the premature hype we see today, capable of generating individualised blackmail material at mass scale, for instance[14]. As with NLP, existing systems are able to spot the 'tells' of GANs whose footprint they are aware of from seeing their previous work. But any new system presents a much bigger challenge[15]. We can expect a future world complicated by credible video disinformation.

Dynamic Content Optimisation (DCO)

Contrary to our wishful thinking, the West has not won the Ukraine information war[16]. Large parts of the world embrace the Russian narrative, or give it moral equivalency. If the info war is still underway, the way it is fought counts. It has more precedent in the advertising technology field (adtech) than in propaganda wars of the past.

Dynamic creative optimisation (or DCO) is a real-time digital version of the old Woolworth's pick'n'mix. It is a standard form of digital content marketing in which the material is continually flexed via automated A/B testing of different versions - such that instead of everyone seeing the same advert, each user is served the exact optimal combination of images, colours and copy to maximise their propensity to buy.

In social media distribution - think *Facebook's* Ads Manager for instance, which is a standard small business tool, or programmatic advertising exchanges in general - machine learning and AI are used to serve content at scale, and optimise the audience responsiveness for each cohort or individual. That's what is now going on already in the information war.

Each side has deployed social media and adtech at scale, both formally and informally, turning the info-war around Ukraine conflict into a real-time, 24/7 conflict of competing narratives on *Twitter, TikTok, Signal* and text messages. *Twitter* accounts cover the Ukraine side, such as OSINT technical and Blue Sauron, presenting daily footage of effective war fighting. Video assets are sliced and diced as assiduously as in any other genre, informed by the storytelling tropes of social and digital marketing and assisted by the AI production tools in smartphones. Transformers (another term in NLP) can write news articles and social media posts by the thousand on either side.

Ukraine overwhelmed Russian social media efforts in the period March-April 2022, with slick, well-edited video clips of apparently successful strikes on Russian armour. They used music, which amplifies performance in social video. Google research on *YouTube* videos, has shown that flipping the narrative so that the best action is played first and then the story recaps from the beginning is the most effective at attention and retention. This kind of approach is also visible in the Ukraine video. Western countries similarly won early advantage by pre-empting Russian narratives with early release of intelligence to neutralise whatever Kremlin disinformation - a notable shift from relative silence around the Crimean invasion narratives of 2014. It was a common observation that Putin's techniques had been used against him.

But if creativity is the killer app, it is not one uniquely iterated on the Western side. Russian social media noticeably raised its game by May 2022, putting out slick video of its own drone strikes, or images of groups of soldiers each operating their own consumer drones. A St Petersburg 'troll factory'[17] pumps out social content to amplify Kremlin narratives, manipulate polls and 'brigade' discussion, borrowing techniques from Isis before it, according to a UK government report in May.

Ukraine as Move 37

These were four paradigm shifts. As Will Knight wrote in WIRED: "With vast amounts of data becoming available to intelligence analysts, new tools will help them sift and interpret it all—but they will introduce new risks, too." These risks include the actual development of autonomous AI-driven weapons systems; the Russians may have such a drone in the KUB-BLA already[18]. There have probably been other AI tools that we don't know about. As quantum computing[19] comes on stream within the decade, the ability to crack codes - 'encryptogeddon' - process information and create synthetic data at scale will again rise.

With the speed, precision, mass personalisation and optimisation of AI, whether on the real battlefield or the information space, what is happening in Ukraine is the prototype for AI wars of the future.

Notes

[1] Quoted in WIRED, May 2022

[2] https://www.reuters.com/business/aerospace-defense/exclusive-us-plans-sell-armed-drones-ukraine-coming-days-sources-2022-06-01/

[3] https://www.csis.org/analysis/russia-probably-has-not-used-ai-enabled-weapons-ukraine-could-change

[4] https://www.techradar.com/uk/news/captcha-if-you-can-how-youve-been-training-ai-for-years-without-realising-it

[5] https://www.satellitetoday.com/government-military/2022/04/26/intelligence-community-is-rapidly-delivering-commercial-satellite-imagery-to-ukraine-nga-official-says/

[6] Davies & Steward, RUSI, May 2022

[7] https://rd.nytimes.com/research/computer-vision

[8] https://blog.hootsuite.com/simon-kemp-social-media/

[9] https://theaisummer.com/transformer/

[10] https://primer.ai/news/wired-as-russia-plots-its-next-move-an-ai-listens-to-the-chatter/

[11] https://peoiews.army.mil/titan-brings-together-systems-for-next-generation-intelligence-capabilities/

[12] https://www.wired.com/story/zelensky-deepfake-facebook-twitter-playbook/

[13] https://www.theregreview.org/2021/08/14/saturday-seminar-responding-deepfakes-disinformation/

[14] https://www.nscai.gov/wp-content/uploads/2021/03/Full-Report-Digital-1.pdf

[15] https://www.media.mit.edu/projects/detect-fakes/overview/

[16] https://www.theatlantic.com/ideas/archive/2022/04/russian-propaganda-zelensky-information-war/629475/

[17] https://www.theguardian.com/world/2022/may/01/troll-factory-spreading-russian-pro-war-lies-online-says-uk

[18] https://www.csis.org/analysis/russia-probably-has-not-used-ai-enabled-weapons-ukraine-could-change

[19] https://www.ft.com/content/a8204a7d-2922-4944-bdff-5449a8f3aee9

About the contributor

Dr Alex Connock is a Fellow at Said Business School, Oxford University and co-director of the AI for Business postgraduate programme. His book *Media Management and Artificial Intelligence* is coming out in November (Routledge.). He is also Professor in Practice at Exeter University and Head of Department in Creative Business at the National Film and Television School.

Agile intelligence in the Ukraine - Net russkim!!

Russia's nihilistic invasion of Ukraine has sparked a new paradigm for democratic intelligence operations in war. Western intelligence officials communicating to and with their public, with unprecedented openness, often through the fourth estate, have been a great counter to Russian propaganda and military aggression, writes Dr Paul Lashmar of City University London

Nearly a year before the Russian invasion of Ukraine the United States intelligence community was openly warning of a possible attack. In one report in April 2021, the BBC quoted a senior US official in Russia as saying the Kremlin could intervene militarily, to enable the pro-Russian separatist Donetsk and Luhansk People's Republics to expand. The report noted: 'The warning comes after weeks of increased fighting between Ukrainian government forces and Russian-backed rebels. America says it's deeply concerned that Russia has deployed more troops on its border with Ukraine than at any time since 2014, when Russian forces seized control of Crimea' (Lobel, 2021).

In the following months the US warnings increased in severity and frequency. On 12 November 2021 *The Daily Mirror* stated, 'The US is said to have raised the alarm with its EU allies that a possible invasion could be looming, and the intelligence is reportedly based on details that have not been disclosed' (Walker 2021).

Meanwhile, over 100,000 Russian troops massed on Ukrainian's borders but fortunately US Intelligence weren't taken in by Putin's feints, like the supposed withdrawal of some forces, nor by the Kremlin and Russian diplomats' dismissing invasion claims and repeating these were just military exercises.

The combined resources of Nato, the Five Eyes group, (A signals intelligence network with the agencies of the US, UK, Canada, Australia and New Zealand that intercepts hostile state communication across the world) and Ukraine's own intelligence agencies produced unerringly correct situation reps. Some sceptical journalists have been wrong-footed by their accuracy. On 1 Dec 2021 *The Jerusalem Post* ran an article headlined: 'Despite war clouds, a Ukraine-Russia clash is unlikely - analysis.' It went on: 'It's entirely possible that the rumours of war are all designed, by both sides, to distract and to deter. If that's the case it could just be bluster.' The *Post* was dismissive, thought the logistics of invasion were too complicated, and the huge troop movements just a Kremlin show of power, 'the move from Yelnya to Ukraine would take time and the highways here do not go south, the units would have to traverse Belarus probably to land on Ukraine's approaches to Kyiv'. But that was exactly what happened.

By 10 February 2022, with Russian forces had massed as far north west as Belarus, US officials now said it was a 'distinct possibility' that this would likely be a full-scale invasion. Then on the 24 February 2022, the Russians launched what was meant to be a blitzkrieg from the northern and eastern borders of Ukraine, clearly intending to take the majority of country and impose 'Russianisation'. The next two months are already an epic of Ukrainian resistance and Russian failures and war crimes. British military intelligence has issued useful daily bullet point assessments of Russian progress. They can be found on the UK Ministry of Defence *Twitter* feed.

Reputations redeemed?

In terms of effective strategic warning, the Ukrainian War has allowed Western intelligence agencies to redeem their reputations after their failure over the invasion of Iraq in 2003. Then Western intelligence on alleged 'Weapons of Mass Destruction (WMD)' was used to justify the invasion and to try and persuade the United Nations to authorise military action against Iraq. As General Colin Powell, then US Secretary of State, subsequently admitted, his PowerPoint briefing 'detailing' Saddam Hussein's WMDs, later proved to be based on false information and was a body blow to his hard-won reputation. It did not convince the United Nations either. This time there was no intelligence failure. Intense Western intelligence and military support from 2014 enabled Ukraine to be prepared and act effectively. Their allies have been able to supply and train the Ukrainian military in the latest western weapons and tactics.

Previous political leaders had been fooled by Putin. George W. Bush, then a few months into his presidency, emerged from a 16th-century castle in Slovenia on a summer's day in 2001 to say he had looked into the eyes of Putin. 'I was able to get a sense of his soul,' Bush said. 'I found him to be very straightforward and trustworthy' (Campbell 2021, 13). Tony Blair thought that Putin was a man of his word and wanted to move Russia into the Western sphere. Not able to do so on his terms, Putin changed tactics. Planning to take all Ukraine was begun, as Putin ordered cyber warfare against the 2016 US election to support Trump and also to encourage the British electorate to vote for Brexit.

Biden's (right) call on Ukraine

As with President Volodymyr Zelenskyy of Ukraine, the right leader at the right time makes a big difference to success. President Biden has to take credit for getting the call right on American leadership in support of Zelenskyy. Trump's admiration of the former KGB colonel Putin suggests he would have distanced the US from action in Ukraine. Biden has been in stark contrast to Trump, stonewalling Putin from the beginning of his Presidency. From Biden's experience in the Obama administration, he took the view Putin had no soul and was a killer.

Learning from the intelligence failure of the surprise seizure of Crimea in 2014, the Ukrainian military and intelligence services have reformed with the primary aim of stopping any further invasion. Unlike the Russians, the Ukrainians refined an agile response to warfare, on the ground and in their intelligence operations, making the best of their smaller arsenal.

Western intelligence goes open!

But something else was new with the Ukraine war. The idea that intelligence should not be only cloak and dagger and seen only a 'need to know' basis has receded. Obviously, the agencies are not releasing the sources of their information or whether it is gained from Signals intelligence, human intelligence, photo intelligence and electronic intelligence . However, the US Intelligence sharing of pre-emptive 'pre-buttals' forced the Russians into strategic lies which have discredited them. The Kremlin has been thrown by this assertive approach. AFP reported on 21 November 2021, 'Kremlin spokesman Dmitry Peskov on Sunday slammed the United States for driving "hysteria" over a possible Russian invasion of Ukraine, after Western countries accused Moscow of a troop build-up near the ex-Soviet country'.

The motor for the new openness has been accountability, technology, crowdsourcing and Open Source Intelligence (OSINT). That just about every citizen, even in Russia, has access to internet and social media makes them a potential intelligence analyst. There are easily available programmes that aide analysis data. Overhead images are provided by commercial satellites like Maxar, so you can plot Russian military movements and much more on your home computer.

Belling the Cat

Leading on this innovation has been Bellingcat, the Netherlands-based investigative journalism group, that specialises in fact-checking and OSINT (see Ch 15 in this book). It was founded by British former blogger Eliot Higgins in July 2014. Some of their methods and capabilities are the envy of intelligence agencies. For MI6, the CIA and other Western agencies getting human intelligence from within authoritarian regimes is a tough call. Bellingcat crowdsourcing can call upon hundreds of citizen experts and often from techno-activists within those regimes who can send information through the dark web or by using VPNs and encryption.

Even before the 2022 invasion, Russia has provided some of the best targets to test Bellingcat's investigative innovations. On 17 July 2014 Malaysia Airlines Flight MH 17, a passenger flight from Amsterdam to Kuala Lumpur, was shot down while flying over eastern Ukraine. All 283 passengers and 15 crew members died after the Boeing 777 was hit by a missile. In a press conference, Russian officials claimed Ukrainian forces had destroyed the flight and presented radar data, expert testimony and a satellite image. Over a period of months Bellingcat destroyed the Russian case and showed the aircraft had been shot down by a Russian army BUK Ground to Air missile even identifying the crew and those in the chain of command who issued the order to launch the missile.

Bellingcat have also been effective in revealing Russian covert operations both within and outside Russia. They were able to identify the assassination team from the Main Intelligence Directorate (GRU) who came close to fatally poisoning former KGB officer Sergei Skipral and his daughter Yulia in the UK town of Salisbury in 2018 but killed an unconnected woman instead. As shown in the remarkable Navalny documentary (2022), Bellingcat worked with the Russian opposition leader to expose the GRU's poisoning plot that nearly killed him. After the documentary was recorded Navalny returned to Russia and was jailed.

Invasion and co-operation

Ukraine was getting real time intelligence from allies and this greatly assisted military successes. It is widely thought that the targeting information that enabled the Ukrainians to sink the Russian Black Sea flagship Moskva on 14 April 2022 came from Western intelligence. Unlike with the WMD in claims, the quality news media in democratic countries has largely reacted well to emergence of the pro-Ukraine intelligence community operating in the public sphere, as they accredited trust with reliable reports.

Russian intelligence, nul points

The intelligence failure of this war has been Russia, a by-product of deep state corruption. It seems fearful officials and generals fed completely inaccurate information to Putin about the state of military readiness and morale of the Ukrainian people and the Russian military. That was a complete underestimation in the first case and an overestimation in the latter. This has cost; the lives of tens of thousands of Russian soldiers, huge quantities of destroyed military equipment and Russia's global reputation. Much worse, it has cost the lives of thousands of Ukrainians, including many civilians, while others have suffered maiming, torture, rape, looting, forced migration and the loss of their home and the destruction of their cities. One hopes that the new era of democratic intelligence will further assist Ukraine to reinstate their civilised democracy, free of Putin's evil empire. There are questions that remain about the West's support for Ukraine prior to 2021. Why did the British and other governments refuse to supply Ukraine with quality and quantity of weapons after 2014 that might have deterred the invasion? Was that an intelligence or political failure? There was a belief that it would antagonise Putin, rather than he was planning to invade all along. The West read him wrong. And why on earth did Germany and France evade sanctions to sell weapons to Russia? Who did they think he would use them against?

Bibliography
Campbell, Matthew (2021) 'Branding him a killer won't bother Putin' *Sunday Times*, 18 April. p.13

Lobel, Mark (2021) Ukraine Report, *BBC World Service News*, 9 April 2021

Walker, William (2021) 'The US is said to have raised the alarm with its EU allies that a possible invasion could be looming, and the intelligence is reportedly based on details that have not been disclosed', *The Daily Mirror*, 12 November

About the contributor
Paul Lashmar is a former Head of the Department of Journalism at City, University of London (2019-2021). He is a Reader in Journalism, and his research interests include media freedom, investigative journalism, intelligence-media relations and organised crime reporting. He has been an investigative journalist since 1978 and has been on the staff of *The Observer*, Granada Television's *World in Action*, current affairs series and *The Independent*.

Can a cyberwar fairy story have a happy ending?

Former Fleet Street editor and foreign correspondent Paul Connew looks at how the Ukraine War exemplifies the importance of cyberspace as a weapon alongside the battles on the ground

'Once upon a time', which is how the best and worst fairy stories begin, grizzled old foreign correspondents like me thought we could spot a happy ending. Technology. The dawn of the internet, the age of the mobile phone with camera, the emergence of social media; the weapons by which wartime propaganda, censorship and lies (or fake news as we so often now dub it) could be defeated and truth and transparency emerge the glorious victors.

Were we right? Well, yes, but only up to a point, dear reader. The Ukraine war, the biggest war in Europe since World War Two, indeed represents the best and the worst of those fairy tale hopes, the brave and the beautiful, the brutal and ugly sides of journalism's Brave New World.

If the Ukraine War has been a modern television war, often in real time, then it is arguably even more the internet war, the social media war and a war where the old enemies of propaganda, censorship and atrocity on a horrific scale have refused to lie down and die or surrender to technological truth. Doubtless, deserved awards will flow for UK broadcasters, although better recognition for brave local 'fixers' might also be in order.

A fair fight?

In what has often resembled an information war title fight between the underdog challenger, Ukraine's Volodymyr Zelenskyy and his heavyweight Russian opponent Vladimir Putin, it is the former professional TV comedian and actor who has landed the heavier blows, harnessing his broadcasting skills to Ukraine's nimble flair for exploiting social media platforms. Aided by Ukrainian civilians brilliantly mobilising that technology to aid an honourable propaganda cause, spreading footage of the realities of war and Russia's brutal and frequently barbaric war crime contempt for the Geneva Convention and every other conflict zone decency. Many tech-savvy Ukrainian civilians joined their nation's "IT Army" hacking into and taking down Russian websites with considerable success.

Compared to Moscow, Kyiv's misinformation strategy has largely been limited to exaggerating the count of top Russian generals killed, overall enemy casualty figures and underestimated its own military losses. In the fog of this war, fully accurate figures for the civilian carnage toll are understandably elusive.

Zelenskyy's David and Goliath card

Whether Vladimir Putin and his Kremlin advisers had underestimated Ukraine's capacity for technological counter-attack on the propaganda front along with underestimating its' military prowess and resolve and Zelenskyy's ability to prove an inspirational war leader and iconic international hero is one of the great mysteries of the whole conflict and its global impact way beyond the immediate battlefields.

President Zelenskyy and his team have adeptly played the David v Goliath card, or arguably Rocky Balboa vs Apollo Creed, an image that went down particularly well with an American audience.

Russia: too posh to push propaganda?

Did arrogance and complacency, on top of immoral ambition, undermine Putin's approach to the propaganda dimension of a Ukraine War he considered a relative military walkover which the West wouldn't challenge much beyond ineffectual condemnation at the United Nations and limited, short-lived sanctions?

If so, it was a calamitous misjudgement. At least on much of the world stage. All the more surprising, given Russia under Putin is an old hand at propaganda and cyberwarfare as a major weapon of choice. Remember the Russian troll farms that fought to secure Donald Trump's 2016 US presidential victory and their possible efforts to influence the UK's Brexit referendum the same year, as well as other Western democratic polls.

Two comedic leaders, one serious?

The Kremlin propaganda machine even missed a trick when branding Boris Johnson its 'number one enemy' over his high-profile support for Ukraine and President Zelenskyy personally (a case of a politician who fancies himself as a comedian envying a professional comedian transformed into a widely revered international hero?). Readers of this 'hackademic' book series will know I'm no champion of Boris Johnson as a credible leader, but he does merit genuine respect over his swift and voluble support for Ukraine and condemnation of Putin. Even if his *faux* Churchill rhetoric grated at times.

That said, Kremlin spin doctors appear to have forgotten that, during the 2016 EU referendum campaign, Boris mitigated Russia's illegal 2014 annexation of Crimea and partly blamed the EU for it; a stance that saw him dubbed a 'Putin

Apologist' by politicians and others from both the Left and the Right. Luckily for the prime minister, much of the UK MSM (Mainstream Media) and Opposition party leaders as well as the Kremlin's propaganda brigade haven't reminded him, whether out of memory failure or wartime diplomacy discretion.

Meanwhile some pro-Johnson UK newspapers have too readily swallowed the spin by Boris allies pitching him rather than President Biden as the West's Ukraine war leader. Perish the thought we're talking a useful diversionary counter narrative to the PM's domestic woes like 'Partygate' and the cost of living crisis!

Putin in command?

But before we get carried away with a fairy tale happy ending notion of Putin's total defeat on the information war front, or delude ourselves that the marvels of the internet, the brighter side of social media platforms, modern MSM technology et al have created a Utopia ruled by truth and transparency with black propaganda vanquished and impotent, reality checks are required.

Domestically, Putin (whose state of mind and physical health became a legitimate target for speculation) and Kremlin strategists' information war focus on deception operations, draconian censorship and false narratives continues to work among many millions of ordinary Russian civilians. Even independent opinion polls carried out secretly by courageous Russian academic Maxim Katz reflects that, along with acceptance of Putin's mantra of a limited military operation, not a war, with only military targets being hit and grateful civilians being rescued, or his emotion blackmail false narrative of the "de-Nazification" of a Ukraine apparently run by Hitler revisionists, led by the Jewish Zelenskyy, a man with relatives who perished in the Nazi concentration camps.

Or, to put it another way, perhaps, when Maxim, a Russian opposition politician who has so far avoided jail, and a team of researchers tried to conduct an independent telephone opinion poll on the Ukraine War, 29,400 out of 31,400 called hung up immediately they heard the subject matter!

Shutting down the messengers

Russia has succeeded largely in shutting down its citizens access to online information sources about Ukraine, with a combination of technological censorship and traditional repressive methods such as hefty jail sentences for those who dare to publicly protest or challenge in person or online the official, sanitised version of events.

Before we console ourselves with the thought that's a strategy only working domestically for Putin and his propaganda machine, consider that it's the version being propagated by Russia's key ally, China. The Chinese Communist Party leadership has mobilised its own draconian information control apparatus to largely echo Putin's version and severely restrict its people's access to alternative information sources. Like Russia' state-controlled print and broadcast media,

China's national broadcaster, *China Central Television (CCTV)* and the CPC's print mouthpiece, *People's Daily*, pump out a steady stream of pro-Russian accounts divorced from reality (see Ch 25 in this book). Little chance of the charismatic Zelenskyy's eloquent TV appeals popping up onscreen, unless his words are buried beneath a derogatory voiceover translation.

And further afield …

To a lesser extent, other Russian allies or client states, usually run by censorious, control freak autocrats, have pumped out a depressing acceptance of Putin's dark fairy tale. Even the reluctance of India, supposedly the world's largest democracy, to come out clearly against Russia's aggressive invasion and to side with Ukraine's position has gifted Putin a propaganda bonus beyond India's heavy reliance on Russia energy supplies and longstanding arms deals.

But there are glimmers of domestic hope on the Information War frontline in both Russia and China, albeit largely confined to young, liberal, tech savvy citizens. Open-source online intelligence tools (OSINT) such as used by the highly regarded UK founded Bellingcat (see Ch 15 in this book) along with VPNs (virtual private networks) are much harder to track down and shutdown.

Fukuyama fires warning shots

To end near where we began, Francis Fukuyama, the distinguished US political scientist, economist and historian, began a March 2022 *Financial Times* article with: "The horrific invasion of Ukraine on February 24 has been seen as a critical turning point in world history. Many have said that it definitely marks the end of the post-war era, a rollback of 'Europe whole and free' that we thought emerged after 1991 or, indeed, the end of The End of History'.

While he doesn't entirely buy into that apocalyptic vision, Fukuyama's upcoming new book *Liberalism and its discontents* takes a searching love/hate look at the internet, which he argues was rightly 'initially celebrated for its ability to bypass hierarchical gatekeepers such as governments, publishers and traditional media. But this new world has turned out to have a big downside, as malevolent actors from Russia to QAnon conspiracists in the US have used this new freedom to spread disinformation and hate speech. These trends were abetted in, in turn, by the self-interest of the big internet platforms that thrived not on reliable information but on virality".

Fukuyama certainly has a point. But if nothing else, the Ukraine War horror story is enabling the Tech Titans of Silicon Valley and the traditional MSM to claw back some lost territory and regain a degree of the moral high ground and the importance of essential truth.

About the contributor

Paul Connew is the former editor of the *Sunday Mirror*, deputy editor of the *Daily Mirror* and Mirror Group US bureau chief, and a former foreign correspondent with experience in various conflict zones. He regularly writes and broadcasts on media and political issues for news organisations at home and abroad. Connew has been a contributing author for ten books in this series.

Section three

A LITTLE EUROPEAN WAR?

***

Ireland: Ukrainian refugees welcome; lessons from history

Twelve million have left Ukraine since Putin's troops invaded. Some countries have been especially welcome to them. Ireland remembers its own mass migration in the nineteenth century and greeted Ukrainians with open arms. Jon Williams of RTÉ tells a very personal story of two of them

She had only left Ukraine once before. But 12-year-old Yeva Skaletskaya and her grandmother, Irina, felt they had no choice but to flee the place they called home. Kharkiv in northeast Ukraine is the country's second city. The Russian border is just an hour away by car. A week after Vladimir Putin ordered his 'special military operation' in Ukraine, Yeva and Irina's apartment block was damaged by shelling. The following day, they decided to leave.

By then, many of Yeva's classmates had already gone. Vika was in Germany, Ira in Kremenchuck and Danny was at the Polish border. Yeva did not know where her journey would end, but she and her grandmother set off on a journey in search of safety. The day before the war began, Yeva had begun keeping a diary. "Everyone thinks they know the meaning of the word war," she wrote, "yet hardly anyone knows what that word means for real."

As they travelled across Ukraine, Yeva documented their journey. First stop, a refugee centre in the western city of Uzhhorod. From there, by train to Slovakia and then on to Budapest, Hungary. A volunteer had offered them a place to stay. Before she went to sleep, Yeva updated her diary: "What a gorgeous city [...] emotions were bubbling over, I was in Europe for the first time". Ukraine was on the move. Within two weeks of Russia's invasion, two million people had fled their country – half of them children. Millions more were displaced internally, families forced to say goodbye to fathers and husbands. Most men, ages 18 to 60 were banned from leaving Ukraine in anticipation that they may be drafted to fight on the frontlines. In response, the European Union had enacted unprecedented measures, offering sanctuary to Ukrainian nationals and permanent residents. The 'Temporary Protection Directive' had been drawn up in 2001 in the aftermath of

107

the Balkan wars of the 1990s. It gave them the right to live and work in any of the 27 EU states, as well as Switzerland, Norway, Liechtenstein, and Iceland.

A warm Irish welcome

Triggering it for the first time, European Commission president Ursula von der Leyen said, "All those fleeing Putin's bombs are welcome in Europe. We will provide protection to those seeking shelter and we will help those looking for a safe way home."[1] No country in Europe is further away from Ukraine than Ireland. But by the end of March, just over a month after the war began, Ireland was expecting to house 20,000 refugees[2], ten times the total number who claimed asylum in Ireland in the whole of 2021. By April, 4,000 refugees a week were arriving[3], with the Irish Government preparing to host up to 100,000 Ukrainians. All would have the right to work, access to welfare benefits, healthcare, housing, and education immediately for up to one year, without the requirement to go through lengthy asylum procedures.

Accommodation centres were set up for those with no Irish family or friends. No need for visas, security checks or even passports, with airlines instructed to accept birth certificates and identity cards if those fleeing Ukraine had no travel documents.

Less warm across the Irish Sea

Across the Irish Sea, thousands of British families were also volunteering to house Ukrainian families. A week after the EU opened its doors to those fleeing war, the British Government launched its 'Homes for Ukraine' programme. Families could register to host Ukrainian refugees. But the scheme soon ran into trouble. 'Homes for Ukraine' required Home Office security and background checks and any Ukrainian wanting to travel to Britain would need a visa. The system was slow and bureaucratic. Under 18s travelling alone were not permitted to be hosted under 'Homes for Ukraine'. By May 5th, just 11,100 Ukrainians had arrived in the UK under the scheme[4], out of 65,900 applications, half the number who had arrived in Ireland – a country of five million people, 13 times smaller than the UK.

Two countries, some common history

Separated by two thousand miles, Ireland and Ukraine share a painful past. In 1932-33, up to five million Ukrainians are estimated to have died in the Holodomor famine, a term derived from the Ukrainian words for hunger (holod) and extermination (mor). Its origins lay in the decision by Soviet leader Joseph Stalin to collectivise agriculture in 1929. Individuals were forced to relinquish their land to collective farms. But it led to a fall in production, and chronic food shortages. It also sparked a series of armed uprisings. In some parts of Ukraine, farms, villages, and whole towns were placed on blacklists and prevented from receiving food.

Eighty years earlier, Ireland had endured a similar catastrophe – an Gorta Mór, or the Great Famine. One million people died when the potato crop failed. Many Irish peasants relied on potato farming for their main source of food and income. Without the potato, they had little food to eat and no money to pay their rent, so vast numbers of the Irish poor found themselves hungry and homeless. But what began as a natural catastrophe of extraordinary magnitude was severely worsened by the actions and inactions of the British Government which then ruled Ireland.

Two million Irish men and women fled to escape the famine. Between 1845 and 1855 over 900,000 Irish people arrived in New York alone. Almost half of all immigrants to the United States during the 1840s were Irish. In the words of Ireland's then Taoiseach, Enda Kenny at the White House in 2017, "four decades before Lady Liberty lifted her lamp we were the wretched refuse on the teeming shore"[5].

The Great Famine may be a footnote in 19th century European history, but it is fundamental to an understanding of Ireland's story. Emigration would become a feature of Irish life for decades to come. By 1921, the year of Ireland's independence, its population was barely half of what it had been before the famine. No family was untouched. Stories of suffering would be passed from generation to generation. Of those who died, and those who fled.

So, when the appeal went out for volunteers to house refugees from Ukraine, thousands of Irish families came forward to offer vacant rooms and empty homes, paying back the help others had given Irish men and women of different age. Just weeks after the war in Ukraine began, Dublin was preparing to host its first Saint Patrick's Day festivities in three years. The Covid pandemic had meant pubs were closed and the capital's Patrick's Day parade was cancelled in both 2020 and 2021. While he is the patron saint of Ireland, for many around the world, Patrick is also the patron saint of immigrants.

Safe Refuge in Dublin

In the Dublin suburb of Glasnevin, teachers Catherine Flanagan and Gary Abrahamian had been watching the unfolding horror in Ukraine. They had seen Yeva and her grandmother's story on *Channel 4 News* and decided they had to help. "I teach English and I was taken by the fact that she was writing a diary,"[6] Gary told *RTE*, "I thought 'wow this girl is like Anne Frank' and how terrible that is in 2022, but isn't it wonderful that she is writing a story that needs to be told". Irina, Yeva's grandmother, jumped at the opportunity. With no passport, she could not travel to Britain. Ireland became her lifeline.

United?

On a Friday night, a week before St Patrick's Day, Catherine and Gary waited at Dublin airport for the arrival of Ryanair flight FR1024 from Budapest. Pupils at their schools had painted posters in blue and yellow. One read 'welcome to

Ireland', another 'welcome Yeva'. For Catherine and Gary the wait seemed endless. Finally, after a journey that had taken them across a continent, and lasted a whole week, the airport doors opened, and Yeva and Irina were greeted by their new Irish family. A home away from home. Yeva could finally relax: "I feel safe," she said.

Yeva and Irina are not alone. The United Nations estimates more than 12m people have fled their Ukrainian homes since the conflict began. More than six million have left for neighbouring countries and at least another 6.5million people are thought to be displaced inside the war-torn country itself[7]. Millions of families separated by trauma, pain and anguish.

Just a week after arriving in Ireland, Yeva found herself immersed in the full Irish experience. Two centuries earlier, Saint Patrick had arrived in Ireland as a migrant. So, on the streets of Dublin, on Paddy's Day 2022, it was fitting that yellow and blue, the colours of the Ukrainian flag, were as prominent as Irish green. And in the crowd, watching Ireland's first Saint Patrick's Day Parade in three years, was one of its newest residents: Yeva Skaletskaya.

That evening, she returned home and again opened her diary. "I will write news from Kharkiv and my life in Ireland," Yeva says. "The name of my book is 'War (in 2022: Through the eyes of a child)' and I think I will finish this book when (the war) stops."

Notes
[1] Von der leyn
[2] Irish Times 20.3.22
[3] Irish Examiner 10.3.22
[4] EuroNews 5.5.22
[5] https://www.rte.ie/news/2022/0313/1286184-ukrainian-girl-diary/
[6] https://data2.unhcr.org/en/situations/ukraine

About the contributor
Jon Williams is the Managing Director, News and Current Affairs for RTÉ, Ireland's public service media organisation, and has been since 2017. From 2006-2013 he was the BBC's World News Editor before becoming Managing Editor, International News for ABC in New York.

Abrupt change in American war reporting on Ukraine

Rattled by 9/11, American reporting on the undeclared wars in the Middle East often proved gullible. But the invasion of Ukraine has prompted an abrupt change in war coverage with studied scepticism. Pulitzer Prize winner David Cay Johnston analyses the coverage

Since the British colonial era, war and its lesser cousin, occupation, have been staples of American journalism. By now American journalists ought to be unbridled masters at reporting on armed conflict. Sadly not, with notable exceptions, my review of current news and hoary articles at newspapers.com shows.

For two centuries from the 1750s when Britain and its colonies battled France and its Native American allies for territory up through World War Two and the Korean conflict, the general theme of war coverage was straight forward: America is good, the indigenous are savages, and foreign powers that don't do as Washington commands deserve trouble.

That theme of triumphant American exceptionalism petered out with the undeclared wars in Vietnam, Laos, and Cambodia. Journalists with spine and skill exposed the fabrications ginned up to justify these wars from the fake Gulf of Tonkin attack in Vietnam to the imaginary weapons of mass destruction in Iraq.

The Bright Shining Lie, as journalist Neil Sheehan called it, also laid bare deep divisions in America. Many millions of Americans prefer a lapdog press to watchdog journalism, which Donald Trump exploited by calling journalists "the enemy of the people".

In this century - shocked by the murderous carnage that Osama bin Laden's zealots pulled off on September 11, 2001 - much of American war journalism came wrapped in dishonour. Gullible, even servile, reliance on the official Washington version of events permeated coverage.

Abrupt change

All that changed, abruptly, with the Russian invasion of Ukraine in February 2022. The news coverage has been remarkably smart, contextual, and investigative.

Cable television punditry is another matter. At Rupert Murdoch's *Fox News*, the biggest of America's three major cable television operations, top host Tucker Carlson declared "I'm rooting for Russia." After sensing most Americans were outraged at the invasion, Carlson, who reportedly harbours ambitions of becoming president, and other *Fox* hosts shifted a bit, defending Putin in less stark language.

The Russian invasion, and the valorous Ukrainian resistance, has become a huge domestic political issue. Donald Trump called the invasion "genius," "savvy," and praised Vladimir Putin because "he's taken over a country for $2 worth of sanctions." Just as bizarrely, *Fox News* blames President Joe Biden for the invasion.

The bottom line is that since Trump, America's right-wing pundits and politicians have moved from the red-baiting McCarthy era to aligning with the Kremlin.

Sacre bleu!

Banner headlines about the war

Rarely used banner headlines - stripped across the top of the front page - ran for a month in *The New York Times*. The war led the nightly network newscasts in the USA for almost three months.

Serious efforts to cut through the fog of war were evident as *The New York Times*, *The Wall Street Journal* and other news organizations which made meticulous use of cell phone and street surveillance videos combined with satellite images to document Russian atrocities like the murders in Bucha.

Again, and again Moscow denied reports of gratuitous massacres and bombing civilians fleeing combat. A new generation of American journalists, steeped in digital technology, showed that in this war it's the Kremlin that lies.

European bias

There have been a few cringeworthy moments.

Two days after the invasion began, Charlie D'Agata, a veteran *CBS News* correspondent, reported from Kyiv that "this isn't a place, with all due respect, like Iraq or Afghanistan, that has seen conflict raging for decades. You know, this is a relatively civilized, relatively European - I have to choose those words carefully - city where you wouldn't expect that, or hope, that it's going to happen." D'Agata at least recognized his prejudice.

Old times

Thanks to 1930s news coverage of the Japanese co-prosperity plan and the Nazi invasion of Poland, Americans were primed to expect war before Tokyo bombed Pearl Harbour in 1941. To most Americans the shock and awe of 9/11 came out of nowhere.

When the Twin Towers fell only diligent readers of *The New York Times*, which had reported extensively on al Qaeda, and people who watched a few key television reports on *ABC News* were prepped.

Expecting war

So, what changed? First, the Russian invasion didn't come out of nowhere.

For nearly a decade news reports prepared Americans to expect that Vladimir Putin eventually would send his tanks into the bread-basket that feeds much of Europe and Africa. That Putin has described the collapse of the Soviet Union as the worst political tragedy of the 20th Century is well-known in America.

In 2014 Putin sent Russian soldiers without insignia - his "little green men" - to capture Crimea, denying at the time that they were Russian soldiers. The popular overthrow that year of President Viktor Yanukovych, a Kremlin-backed kleptocrat, and revelations that Trump's 2016 campaign manager, Paul Manafort, was on Yanukovych's payroll, meant that large swaths of Americans understood that Putin wants to dominate what the old Soviet called *The* Ukraine.

In December 2017 I spent a week in Ukraine, the keynote speaker at an investigative journalism conference. Everyone I spoke to from reporters to chambermaids, cabbies, clerks, and waiters seemed resigned to an eventual Russian invasion, especially with Trump in the White House. This year relatives and friends who live in former Soviet satellites have told me, their fear revealed by higher pitched voices, that Russian tanks will roll into Hungary, Moldova, Slovakia, and the Baltic States unless Ukraine defeats Russia.

Contrast this with the fact that few Americans grasped that 9/11 had no military significance, had no idea why "they" would hate us. The George W. Bush administration, exploiting this ignorance, and knowing that fear is a mind killer, persuaded 80% of Americans that Saddam Hussein and Osama bin Laden were allies. The success of that preposterous lie, and the ineffective efforts by news organizations to set the record straight, remains an enduring stain on American journalism.

Honesty pays off

Second, in 2021 a major change took place in how the executive branch of the American government dealt with military information. Instead of Tonkin Gulf and Iraq WMD lies, the Biden administration played it straight. A steady flow of reports by military and diplomatic correspondents last fall made clear that the Russian army wasn't doing much to encrypt its communications. Cell phone calls that Russian grunts made home to mama were easily monitored, revealing discontent with meal packets that expired as long ago as 2002.

Because intelligence assessments given on background to American reporters proved reliable the Biden administration earned trust and goodwill with journalists. This was a sharp turn from the "alternative facts" Trump administration, the cautious Barack Obama administration, and the aggressive George W. Bush who tried to intimidate the executive editor and the publisher of *The New York Times* with threats of prosecution and even execution unless they toed the official line on Middle East war coverage.

Third, no American troops are engaged in Ukraine. The artillery, drones and missiles given to Ukraine are dropped short of the border in Poland and other Nato countries. The aid so far has come to about ten times Ukraine's pre-invasion military budget, a fact that gets little to no mention in American news reports.

Fourth, Putin's brutality in gratuitously levelling apartment buildings, hospitals, schools, and even fleeing convoys of civilians has sparked worldwide revulsion. Only the better news organizations, however, have reported that Putin employed these same terroristic techniques in Chechnya, Georgia, and Syria.

Youthful, journalistic, suspicions

Fifthly, the Russian invasion comes as a seismic shift in economic and social attitudes is spreading among Americans under 40. The economic turmoil of this century and the drawn-out occupations of Afghanistan and Iraq, combined with stagnant wages, is challenging the "greed is good" policies that began four decades ago under Ronald Reagan.

Sixthly, American journalism has long chronicled the dubious activities of Putin and his oligarchs, especially the funding of Western politicians like former German Chancellor Gerhard Schröder, France's fascist leader Marine Le Pen, and Donald Trump's real estate enterprises That Putin and the younger oligarchs form the world's largest and best financed criminal gang is not news to the half of Americans who comprise the Millennials and Gen Z generations born since 1981, including those who are now journalists. A majority reject capitalism and oppose billionaire wealth at home and abroad, surveys show.

American journalists love underdogs. The success and valour of Ukrainian citizen soldiers taking on the Russian army perfectly fits the narrative of the good guys taking on the evil invaders. That Ukraine's president is a charming and fearless advocate who talks straight and talks to reporters has made Vladimir Zelenskyy a household name in the U.S.

Reports from the war zone have been remarkable for the caution in handling claims by all sides. When Ukraine said it sank the *Moskova*, the Russian flag ship on the Black Sea, American news reports carefully noted the lack of independent verification until video surfaced of the sinking and Moscow acknowledged the loss.

The Pentagon told reporters on background that American intelligence was behind the Moskova sinking and the killing of a half dozen Russian generals. That news struck me as unnecessarily provocative bragging.

Biden evidently felt the same way. He told the Pentagon brass to knock it off.

About the contributor

David Cay Johnston is a Pulitzer Prize-winning investigative reporter, formerly with *The New York Times*, a best-selling author, and a press critic. A broadcast chain shut down after he exposed its news manipulations, a unique event in American history. He is co-founder of the non-profit news service DCReport.org. Since 2009 Johnston has taught at Syracuse University College of Law. He is a former president of the 6,000-member Investigative Reporters & Editors (IRE).

'You've been framed Mr Putin'

A report on the observations and surprises, noted by UK university students undertaking journalism degrees at Leeds Trinity University, during our joint exploration of differently styled initial attempts to control meanings about the war in Ukraine. Their tutor Dr Carolyn Jackson Brown takes up the story

Our first surprise was that the war was over, almost as soon as it had started. Or so it seemed as we heard about Putin's rescue package, not just with tanks but now talks, according to *Russia Today's* Western facing TV news output on 24 February. My second year Journalism in Context class had been exploring how meanings are constructed and framed and then, checking out the breaking news in class that day, *even though we were supposed to be analysing the content*, we were actually taken in by this parallel version of unfolding events. The TV trope of the studio news reader with scrolling red strap line beneath was the same as ours, but after just ten minutes it seemed as if we should switch back to the BBC to hear from them that their framing of the 'invasion' of Ukraine had been overplayed. Of course, once I swapped the classroom screen back from state-controlled RT to UK public service broadcasting output it became obvious that their messaging had been as far removed from ours, as East is from West. That perspective shift, and then back again, took us all by surprise. Not that Russia would have a different rhetoric but that, temporarily, it seemed *common sense* to us that Ukraine was politically sick and that Russia were doing the right thing.

My undergraduates were able to observe propaganda at first hand. Both channels' coverage was dressed in the same clothes, with seemingly identical footage, reassuring newsreaders addressing the camera in their reliable studio setting, and the familiar ticker tape scrolling with the latest facts and figures. All so easy to absorb. However, the contrast between the two perspectives was so powerful from these legacy-style broadcasters that even us de-constructionists could barely tell truth from a lie. What did they do next? The students immediately reached for their phones 'to check'.

So, who to trust?

It may surprise readers to note that, even within a current cohort of journalism trainees, their preferred means of finding out what they might need to know, is often via *TikTok*. For others their consumption of news is 'whatever is trending on *Twitter*' although some do follow the accounts of well-respected professional journalists, which of course we encourage. Mostly they wake up each morning to scroll on whichever platform takes their fancy, possibly consuming curated content via, for example, *Apple News*, or for breaking stories most of our cohorts still go to *Twitter* with just a few using *Facebook*.

Different platforms, different stories?

Previously, this cohort had been looking at the delivery systems that have disrupted legacy news broadcasting, so we decided, as a sort of co-creation project, to evaluate 'what was going on in Ukraine' through each person's preferred social media platform, even if they had never looked for news on it before. We also included a glimpse of *Al-Jazeera* to get a relatively balanced reference point, whose world view was more West than East on this occasion.

Straight away students found the 'Special Military Operation' (the Putin euphemism for war) on *Instagram*, with soldiers showing off around their tanks. There were images of Ukrainian Flags being replaced with Russian ones, as if towns were being liberated from their oppressors. We confirmed later that the versions of these appearing both there and on *TikTok* were recycled 2014 images, and not what they claimed to be at all. We teach this next generation of critically thinking communicators to verify photographs as a vital practice when including user-generated content in their reports. I thought it was interesting that none thought to do so on this occasion though, at the exact point when we were trying to establish what was really going on.

This video, image and caption fakery upset one or two members of the class, who rely on their favourite platforms to provide them with real, albeit performed, content that they think they can trust. The question then arose as to whether the deceptions were being produced by Russian social media influencers simply playing to their own audiences, or through an infiltration of content creators at the behest of the Kremlin, presumably to dishearten and deceive the West. The students seemed to think that older people's legacy media might have issues with set views or partisanship (only their parents watch the news on the television or read the *Daily Mail* for example) but clearly they weren't expecting 'fake news from the Russians' to turn up in their smartphones at all, especially via their beloved *Insta* or *TikTok*.

Stranger than fiction?

In the old broadcast media days, in whichever global territory, media producers could shape identities, potentially framing anyone as a villain or a hero, through edited print or onscreen representations, and tell stories about these 'others' to an audience of 'us'. Just by leaving an awkward pause on the end of a sentence in an interview, at the end of a news package or during a documentary, you could for example make one person look guilty but save another, or by not editing out an 'er' imply doubt where there was none, thereby turning fact into fiction. We are all familiar with the use of unfortunate photos of politicians eating bacon sandwiches or yawning to undermine their credibility, which newspapers will do if they are better disposed towards another party or persuasion. These ways of shaping meanings are used all the time to create a safe distance between 'them' and 'us'. But this war in Ukraine is not safe for anyone. Worse still, we, the consumers of curated content, have now become media producers too.

Do the olders know better?

At postgraduate level, prior to making their industry accredited 20-minute documentaries or podcasts, I always ask our masters students to consider the shaping of the public discourse and in particular to critically analyse the media landscape and get a feel for who might be controlling the narrative. The reporting of Ukraine has clearly provided rich material evolving from multiple narratives, which they understand and are able to distinguish better than their younger undergraduates.

We missed a week together whilst the students took their law exams, during which time it became apparent that Putin might justify upping the hostilities in Ukraine if he personally didn't like what was being said about him, especially amongst politicians within Nato countries. It was surprising therefore on the day that we reconvened our class, that the President of the United States chose to suddenly accuse Putin of being a 'war criminal.' My students considered whether his decision to announce that might endanger more lives, so we looked more closely at that story.

The tail wags the dog?

They understand that just as any unregulated content creator anywhere can make up or change what a person says and post it, or quote the comment out of context, sometimes journalists too can put words into other people's mouths. With all of this going on across social media, the echo chambers that pass on breaking news at lightning speed can sometimes also add their momentum in the manner of Chinese Whispers. Once an agreement has become an *accusation* it is much more likely to go viral, for example, then influencers benefit from clickbait heaven, and the public discourse is shaped and takes a turn.

Our Masters students were of the opinion that Biden had outwardly declared that Putin was a 'war criminal' most likely at a press conference. These 'facts' were derived mainly from their normal lunchtime sweep across their phone apps. So, when we looked together at the online article in The *Guardian* (16 March) and watched and re-watched the clip with the sound up, it was fascinating to observe that POTUS had been door-stepped by a journalist in a crowded room after a meeting on another topic. It wasn't even an unguarded corridor conversation; the jostled moment was perhaps, they thought, a little unfair for him, and that framing of meaning almost certainly wasn't on his agenda, they were sure.

Whilst some students felt that it was in the public interest to know immediately what his opinion might be, the questioning technique reminded me of the BBC anecdote about loading questions, often to get a headline, back in the 1990's. If you ask 'When did you stop beating your wife?' you can get a headline implying guilt both ways. Either they tell you when they stopped, or 'they refuse to deny' and we all know, don't we, that there is no smoke without fire. These types of questions reinforce agendas and provide new angles to keep stories fresh, but whether they should be used when potentially lives are at stake, is a conundrum my students weren't convinced about.

Lessons?

Responsible journalism is really important with so many other voices now included in the mix but maybe it is about time everyone developed a bit more media literacy. When our society acts and policies are changed for Ukrainian refugees, because they are 'just like us', every word, every nuance, every shade of meaning should be scrutinised. Perhaps we should not have been surprised that morsels of falsehood were occupying the ostensibly non-political territory of *TikTok* within hours of the tanks rolling in, and that should be a wake up-call for everyone. If our university students can train themselves to spot lies hiding in plain sight, let us hope that the Russian students at least, are learning to do the same.

About the contributor

Dr Carolyn Jackson Brown is a Senior Lecturer in Journalism at Leeds Trinity University and author of *Disability, The Media & The Paralympic Games*, a production study investigating Channel 4's creative & executive decision-makers. Lecturing follows a career in factual broadcast television as a video editor at the BBC.

Reporting Ukraine: more context please!

The Ukraine crisis has showcased our media's strengths whilst simultaneously illustrating some of its chronic weaknesses. In the lead-up to the war historical context was missing and the lazy demonisation of Russia compounded the problem, argues Robin Aitken of the *Daily Telegraph*

Even the sternest critic of the Western media has to concede that it is much preferable to its Russian equivalent. From the first day of the invasion the audience has been offered dramatic and honest, often brave, eyewitness, reporting. In Russia, in contrast, strict censorship means the people have been fed a misleading and distorted narrative whose sole purpose is to bolster a war of aggression. So, whatever our media's faults, we are lucky to live in a country where accurate and truthful information is readily available to all who seek it out (even if many do not). But the professional excellence of what we have been offered shouldn't blind us to underlying weaknesses. Two big questions arise: how well did our media perform in the years running-up to the crisis? And to what extent was the prior Western demonisation of Russia a contributory factor in the tragedy?

War as spectator sport?

First- an observation: for western audiences foreign wars have become a cost-free spectator sport. For many people the Ukraine war is something they actively enjoy as news consumers When the war began the BBC reported huge increases in website traffic and its audiences for traditional radio and TV news; the drama inherent in a violent conflict engages the audience in a way other news events often do not.

The progress of the war was reported in a way akin to a sporting fixture; once we had decided we were on Ukraine's side (an instantaneous decision) the incompetence of Russia's forces and Ukrainian successes were the main themes to emerge. There can be no real quarrel with our partisanship - at this moment Ukraine *does* deserve our support - but the speed with which we, the public, fell-in behind the chosen narrative should give us pause for thought. It demonstrated, very clearly, how public opinion can be quickly marshalled when the mass media unanimously adopts a position on a foreign policy story. The effect is to squeeze out dissenting voices. It becomes difficult to articulate and deliver any contradictory viewpoint and those who try often find their efforts rewarded with scorn and abuse.

Media Russophobia

Part of the reason why the support for Ukraine was so unhesitating and so unstinting was because in the years leading up to the invasion Russia became an all-purpose villain for the liberal-left both in the UK and the US. The exaggerated, and, in my view, frankly delusional, allegations about Russian interference in both the Brexit referendum in 2016 and the election that year in the USA of Donald Trump, was a constant theme in mainstream media coverage from 2016 onwards. This coverage primed public opinion; it encouraged an incipient Russophobia and when Putin launched his invasion in February 2022 it merely added the finishing touch to the portrait of a villainous and untrustworthy country.

The hypothesis that Trump was a Russian stooge and that his victory in 2016 was the result of Kremlin meddling was investigated by special prosecutor Robert Mueller and found to be baloney; it was 'fake news' - an obvious smear invented by Democrats unwilling to accept Trump's victory. As for the idea that Russian 'bots' swung the Brexit referendum - that is foolish nonsense which only the weak minded could possibly swallow: the British people had 40 years to arrive at their considered verdict on whether to stay the EU. The Russian interference story was the invention of diehard Remainers who lost the argument and were determined to de-legitimise the result.

It was, anyway, wholly hypocritical to accuse Russia of wicked interference in our affairs when this is exactly what we (as 'The West') have been doing in so many countries, including Ukraine, for the past century and more. Episodes like Nato's aerial bombardment of Serbia in 1999, the Iraq invasion in 2003, the overthrow of Gaddafi in Libya in 2011 are only the most recent instances of direct Western intervention in other countries. You might - if you are a convinced liberal interventionist in the Blair mould - approve of all these actions as self-evidently well-intentioned; suffice it to say many people, especially in non-western countries, strongly disagree.

The Maidan Revolution: US inspired?

What is more germane, in this context, is Western, particularly American, involvement in Ukraine's affairs in 2014. In what became known as The Maidan Revolution in 2014, there was clear involvement of US politicians and officials in events which led to the overthrow of the pro-Russian Ukrainian President Viktor Yanukovych. It was street protests, not the ballot box, which toppled Yanukovych's regime, although his election - in 2010 - was viewed by most international observers as fair. It was not coincidental that the Russian seizure of Crimea and its incursions into eastern Ukraine came shortly after Maidan; the Kremlin was alarmed to see yet another of its former possessions joining the Western bloc.

There are influential figures in Washington who have never made any secret of the fact that weakening Russia power and influence has been, and remains, a US foreign policy objective. In 1992 a draft policy penned by the under-secretary of state for defence policy, Paul Wolfowitz, leaked; it stated the ultimate objective of US foreign policy should be to establish a uni-polar world with America as the only super-power. Russia presents a substantial obstacle to achieving that.

The Maidan Revolution, and the toppling of Yanukovych, was an obvious defeat for Russia and a victory for US foreign policy hawks; without Ukraine in its orbit Russia is considerably weakened. I believe that 'Western values', encompassing free and fair elections, the rule of law, a respect for human and property rights, are morally correct; these values are the foundation stone of 'The West'. But we must always try to understand the viewpoint countries we see as enemies, like Russia. Anyone with any knowledge of Russian history knows there are underlying national neuroses which shape the country. Firstly, the fundamental question of identity: is Russian essentially European and Western or is it an East and Asian power? Secondly the question of borders: the largest country in the world by land mass has no natural borders in the west and southwest (the north and east are different). Thirdly the 'nationalities question'; Russia has the characteristics more of an empire than a 'country' because of the 120 different ethnic groups that live within its borders; the Kremlin knows nationalist instincts in these groups pose a threat to its territorial integrity.

The 'National Question'

In 1913 Stalin, then living in Vienna, wrote a short treatise 'Marxism and the National question' which formulated a solution whereby Russia's many 'nationalities' could be subsumed in the Marxist super-state. The underlying 'national question' proved highly combustible and in 1989 was the trigger for the collapse of the USSR; national minorities asserted their identity and broke free.

Today's Russia is the inheritor of this underlying instability which, in combination with persistent fears about its borders and uncertainty about its true identity have created a witches brew which has infected Putin, and now the whole country, with a deep paranoia about the future. Ukraine embodies all Russia's deepest insecurities; geographically it is in the west, it is a border region and its population mix includes many Russians

Did the West miss the boat?

There was a moment, perhaps, in the 1990s when the West had a golden opportunity to save Russia from itself. The country was economically weak and America and its allies might then have intervened with generosity as they did after the Second World War when Germany and the devastated nations of Europe were restored to health by the Marshall Plan. No such generosity was extended to Russia in the 1990s; instead it descended into a lawless and brutal period best categorised as 'robber capitalism'. Meanwhile most of the formerly subject nations of eastern Europe joined Nato; Russian paranoia was supercharged as a result. There has been very little effort from our media to try to tell this story instead, from 2016 until the present, Russia has been painted as an ogre.

Who is to blame? Putin or the West?

The war in Ukraine is not the media's fault nor the fault of our governments ; the blame lies squarely with President Putin. But both the media, and our politicians, should have done more to understand Russia's anxieties. Britain's foreign policy has been driven by hard-liners in Washington who cast Russia as the eternal enemy a view never properly scrutinised or challenged by our media. Furthermore, our media enthusiastically promoted the (absurd) fictions of the US Democratic party and Remainers in Britain. When the Ukrainian government was overthrown in 2014 we were supposed to cheer the fact - even though, by the standards of east European elections Yanukovych's government was legitimate.

Ukraine and Russia are now the focus of obsessive media attention: where was that focus five, ten or twenty years ago? I believe Ukraine must, as a matter of both morality and natural justice, be allowed to determine its own future; Putin has put his country firmly in the wrong. But how much better would it have been if our media had been paying attention to Russia's concerns twenty years ago? Had we shown more understanding of its anxieties perhaps this tragedy could have been avoided.

About the contributor

Robin Aitken MBE was a BBC reporter for 25 years, finally for the *Today* programme. He now works as a freelance concentrating on media matters especially for the *Daily Telegraph*. His latest book is *The Noble Liar* (Biteback, 2020).

Lies damned lies and Putin's propaganda Why do the Russians fall for it?

Professor Ivor Gaber of the University of Sussex looks not just to what's happening with the Russian media, but also to social psychology, to try to understand why the Russian population is 'taken in' by the blatant untruths told to them by Vladimir Putin and his media acolytes

It's been one of the more puzzling, but also sinister, aspects of the invasion of Ukraine by Russian forces. When Ukrainians were telling family members in Russia about their lives under bombardment, they were being told that it was just not true, or that the bombardment was probably coming from the Ukrainian side as a 'false flag' event, or that the Russians were engaged in a legitimate act of self-defence.

Why they believe it?

So how is it that such a large percentage of Russians, if we can believe the opinion polling, have come to be so brainwashed? The answer is threefold.

First, there is a grand narrative that has long gripped the Russian imagination - that Putin reiterated on 'Victory Day' 2022' - which is that the country has always been under threat from European expansionism. As there is no natural geographical barrier protecting Russia from the West so, over the centuries, the Swedes, the Poles, Napoleon's army and, most recently, Hitler's Wehrmacht have swept eastwards. The Nazi invasion in 1940 represented the apotheosis of this fear as the German army raced across the West European Plain to occupy much of Ukraine and Western Russia, before finally being repelled by the Red Army - but at huge cost, with Russian losses of civilians and military estimated at over five million.

The grand narrative continues with the assertion that Russia, almost alone, defeated Nazi Germany in 'The Great Patriotic War' - and that the threat of invasion from the West, now in the form of Nato , remains, with Ukraine as its cat's paw. Prior to the collapse of Communism, Russia (or the Soviet Union as it then was) had a buffer of Eastern European states to protect it, but as these states were drawn into Nato, Russia was left feeling isolated and threatened.

Into this toxic mix the Kremlin has added the suggestion that the Nazis were never really defeated and, because of the key role that the ultra-right Azov Brigade has played in Ukrainian politics, then Ukraine is a Nazi state. Hence, all Ukrainians are either actual or potential Nazis. This is one explanation for the barbarities that Russian soldiers have been inflicting on both Ukrainian soldiers and civilians.

Media transmission

The second explanation for this brainwashing is that this grand narrative has been reiterated and amplified by the Russian media which, during Putin's rule, has lost almost all its independence so that now there is no major broadcasting service, or newspaper or news website, that is not simply reproducing Kremlin propaganda about the 'special military operation'. Should any journalist stray from the official line, they face heavy fines and up to 15 years in prison.

The last major bastion of independent media was the *Novaya Gazeta* newspaper which suspended operations just four days after the invasion began, having received its second warning from the government censor for allegedly breaching the so called 'foreign agent law' - the mechanism used to shut down critical media. The other main sources of independent news - the liberal radio station *Ekho Moskvy*, the TV *Rain* channel and *Meduza* news website - had already been closed. Hence, the main source of news for most Russians during the war has been the state-run TV channels which have done little other than pump out up to fifteen hours of propaganda every day.

Nor has social media provided an effective alternative source of news, with *Twitter* and *Facebook* both being blocked and *Instagram* restricted, although it could still be accessed via virtual private networks (VPNs). *Instagram* has 38 million regular users in Russia, the third most popular social media outlet. *WhatsApp* is the most popular with 81 million users and the Russian platform *Vkontake*, at 76 million, is in second place[1]. The extent that *WhatsApp* could be a source of unofficial news about the war is difficult to ascertain since the network is encrypted; but we do know that *Vkontake* can be relied on not to carry material that substantively challenges the Kremlin line.

You can fool some of the people some of the time

The third explanation is perhaps the most sinister and, in some ways, the most difficult to combat - and that is how relatively easy it is to get people to believe fake news and disinformation, and how difficult it is to persuade them that these beliefs are false. President Trump's success in implanting his fake narrative about the 'stolen election' into the American mainstream is a case in point. Despite the fact that the lie was so blatant that it should never have gained any traction, it is nonetheless still believed by one in three Americans; and this, despite the fact that the US media (legacy and social) do not face any of the sort of restrictions that have wiped-out independent media in Russia.[2]

The fact that people appear to be so ready to believe stories that on any rational basis are clearly false, and to accept the 'alternative realities' they thrive on, has been attracting growing interest from academic researchers - experimental psychologists in particular. Whilst there is no one simple explanation, the insights they offer can help better understand this phenomenon (though it is worth noting in passing, that fake news is not a new development, long predating the rise of social media).

Saving our brain power. What Experimental psychology teaches us

The social psychologists' starting point is the notion that we are all 'cognitive misers'; in other words, just as humans are programmed to conserve their physical strength - taking the lift instead of the stairs - so too do we seek to conserve our mental strength as well. Hence, in order to process the vast amounts of data that we are daily being exposed to, we tend to construct mental maps, or frames, which help us understand the world. In the days of the Cold War, for example, there was a very simple map which explained international conflicts in terms of 'our side' being right and the 'other side' being wrong. With the ending of the Cold War that global map faded for most people, although there are still some - mostly on the far left - who cannot quite shake off the notion that in all foreign conflicts the Russians (the Soviet Union, as was) are the good guys and the Americans/Nato are the bad.

Information that challenges our mind maps causes cognitive dissonance, which occurs when we try to rewire our brains to accept something that, until that point, we have always believed was untrue; in this example it would be requiring Russians to see themselves as the aggressor and Ukraine as the victim. So, this information is rejected and other sources are looked for which will confirm what we have always believed - this is the so-called 'confirmation bias'.[3]

But the problem of disinformation doesn't end there

Researchers have found that even if the Russian public were to get access to reports that challenged the Kremlin narrative, the reports would probably be rejected; for apart from 'confirmation bias' there is 'source contamination' as well. This would arise because the Russian reader might well regard the source of the discordant information - be it foreign media, foreign governments or even dissident individuals –as contaminated. So, because they were unsympathetic to any messages that appeared to challenge their current 'mind map', they would either just not notice the messages, or more likely, not retain any memory of them. Indeed, there is evidence of a so-called 'backfire effect' in which partisan audiences did not just disbelieve rebuttals but the rebuttal actually increased the intensity of their belief in the original lie.[4]

Repetition, repetition. repetition

Another factor involved in the embedding of false information is known as 'fluency' - the easier the information is to understand, the more likely people will believe it's true. In other words, if the information fits your world view - e.g. that if you believe that Nato is an ongoing threat to Russia - it is easier to accept that Ukraine is simply Nato's pawn and hence it is legitimate to invade the country as an act of 'self-defence'. This is why repetition is so important in the process of constructing an 'alternative reality' - the more you hear something the more likely you are to believe it.[5]

The advertising world knew this long before academia. They coined the phrase 'banging on the bruise' - make a strong initial impact and then every subsequent mention reinforces the original message. As long as the original statement is strong enough, and sufficiently memorable, it will have an impact, particularly among partisans; they will recall that first positive impact every time the lie is repeated even if it is repeated in the process of rebuttal.[6]

When the history of the Russia/Ukraine war comes to be written it won't be just on the battlefield that the victory, will be seen to have been won or lost (or at least claimed), but on the home front as well. This is why the Kremlin is so keen to prevent the Russians people from learning about the realities of the war - both its build-up and context.

There is little doubt that Ukrainians are similarly affected by the psychological processes described above, but the big difference between their support for their government and Russians doing likewise is that there are no restrictions in what Ukrainians can see or read from foreign sources, other than that emanating from Moscow, whilst Russians now have very limited access to foreign news. And, perhaps most important of all, the Ukrainians 'grand narrative' is simply that of the pride in being an independent nation for almost the first time in their history, and the very real fear that this is in danger of being snatched away from them by their overbearing neighbour.

Notes

[1] Statista 2022 'Leading social media platforms in Russia in 3rd quarter 2021' https://www.statista.com/statistics/867549/top-active-social-media-platforms-in-russia/

[2] Swire, Briony, Adam J. Berinsky, Stephan Lewandowsky, and Ullrich K. H. Ecker. 2017. "Processing Political Misinformation: Comprehending the Trump Phenomenon." *Royal Society Open Science* 4 (3): 160802

[3] Taddicken, Monika, and Laura Wolff. 2020. "'Fake News' in Science Communication: Emotions and Strategies of Coping with Dissonance Online." *Media and Communication* 8 (1): 206–17

[4] Begg, Ian Maynard, Ann Anas, and Suzanne Farinacci. 1992. "Dissociation of Processes in Belief: Source Recollection, Statement Familiarity, and the Illusion of Truth." *Journal of Experimental Psychology: General* 121 (4): 446–58.

[5] Reber, Rolf and Unkelbach, Christian 2010 "The Epistemic Status of Processing Fluency as Source for Judgments of Truth" published in *Rev Philos Psychol.* Vol 1 (4): 563–581

[6] Garrett, R. Kelly, and Brian E. Weeks. 2013. "The Promise and Peril of Real-Time Corrections to Political Misperceptions." *Proceedings of the 2013 conference on computer supported cooperativedewwork,* 1047–58

About the contributor

Ivor Gaber is Professor of Political Journalism at the University of Sussex and a former broadcast journalist. He has worked in Ukraine training journalists and press officers in the principles and practices of independent journalism.

How the Russia-Ukraine War is (un)reported in China

Dr Yan Wu of Swansea University analyses the reporting of 2022 Russia-Ukraine War in China and finds three themes in Chinese media: the absence of the war, the framing of war as 'conflict', and the promotion of a 'US threat' discourse

China declared a neutral position immediately after Russia's invasion of Ukraine in February 2022. On the one hand, China is Ukraine's top trade partner and has had a strategic partnership with the country since 2011. Ukraine joined China's Belt and Road initiative[1] in 2017 and has since attracted huge amounts of Chinese investment. Before the Russian invasion, Beijing also demonstrated its support 'for the territorial integrity of Ukraine' (Gerasymchuk & Poita, 2018:11). On the other hand, being Russia's long-term ally, China has deepened its relationship with Russia in 2019 to 'a comprehensive strategic partnership of coordination' (Xinhua, 2019) with 'no limits'.

Let's analyse the reporting of the Russia-Ukraine War 2022 by three Chinese state-controlled central media - namely *Xinhua News Agency (Xinhua)*, *China Central Television (CCTV)* and *People's Daily* and evaluate if China's self-claimed 'neutrality' position leads to fair and impartial reporting. These three media organisations are all under the strict control of the Chinese Communist Party's (CCP) and serve as a barometer of China's policies on major domestic and international incidents. Three tropes of Chinese media's reporting can be detected from its reporting since 24 February 2022, namely, the absence of the war; framing the war as 'conflict' and utilizing the war to promote a 'US threat' discourse.

Chinese propaganda control and Mariupol off the radar

Firstly, the media in China is strictly controlled in terms of what can be reported and what is not allowed to be reported about Russia's invasion of Ukraine. Two days before the outbreak of the war, *Beijing News'* international news channel leaked an official instruction on its social media account. In this guidance received from the government, the media in China were instructed to 'not post anything unfavourable to Russia or pro-Western. [...] If using hashtags, only use those started by *People's Daily, Xinhua, or CCTV.*' (China Digital Times, 2022). Another leaked censorship directive on Ukraine shows that the scope of censorship covers all media forms ranging from mainstream media, commercial portals, search engines, short video platforms, and other social media platforms. Overseas Chinese individuals' live streams from the battlefield via social media platform would be suspended as well (China Digital Times, 2022). Jixian Wang, a Chinese entrepreneur living in Odesa in Ukraine, recorded in his *YouTube* Vlog on 7 March that all his Chinese social media accounts were suspended and eventually closed due to his reporting of day-to-day life during the War (Wang, 2022).

The most poignant recent example is on 24 May, when the international media's attention was on the discovery of more than 200 bodies in the rubble of an apartment building in Mariupol. CCTV's international news homepage featured only one item about Ukraine war. This story is entitled "Russian military troops entering Azovstal Steel Plant for mine clearance":

> On 22 May 2022 local time, Russian soldiers used de-mining devices to clear mines, and military bulldozers to clear weapons and building debris in the Azovstal Steel Plant in Mariupol, Donetsk region. According to Russian soldiers, more than 100 explosives have been detonated in the past two days. (CCTV, 2022) (author's translation)

Eighty-nine Chinese characters were used in this story, accompanied by news photos showing Russia solders in demining operation. The atrocities of the war and humanitarian crisis were totally erased from the reporting.

Framing the war as 'conflict'

As defined by Robert Entman, to frame, 'is to select some aspects of a perceived reality and make them more salient in a communicating text' and the ultimate purpose of framing is to define, interpret, and evaluate a problem for suggested 'treatment recommendation' (1993: 52).

It is evident that the Ukraine war was framed as 'conflict' in Chinese media's coverage. A search of key words 'Russia-Ukraine War' in Xinhua's international news dataset (http://www.xinhuanet.com/worldpro/ stories) between 24 February to 24 May generates only four results and all were used in the context of quoting from to the US media. Instead, a search of 'Russia-Ukraine Conflict' in the same dataset generated 480 results. While a search of 'Ukraine invasion' or 'Russia invasion' generated zero results.

It is evident that by framing the war as 'conflict' and making the non-violent aspects of the war salient, Chinese media avoid defining Russia's military operation as an 'invasion', hence avoiding condemning the resulted humanitarian crisis in Ukraine. Such a framing leads to a faulty evaluation of the problem and a recommended solution that fits into the CCP's political agenda.

The US threat

Thirdly, the Chinese media has promoted a 'US threat' discourse via commentaries on the Russia-Ukraine War. In the first three months of the war, *The People's Daily* published in total seventeen commentary articles outlining the newspaper's position. These articles are short (under 500 words), sharp, and each of them is accompanied by a political cartoon. A thematic analysis of these commentary articles reveals the following claims:

1) the US plays an instigator's role in triggering Russia-Ukraine 'conflict';

2) the Russia-Ukraine 'conflict' was one of the most recent US activated global wars aiming to reinforce US hegemony;

3) Nato has been hijacked by the US in the post-Cold War era. Its European members would suffer from this 'conflict', but the war would benefit the American military industry complex.

One cartoon published on the 29 March shows the epitome of this 'US threat' discourse. The image shows a car crash scene witnessed by five men, with the connotation that the two vehicles involved are Russia and Ukraine and the five men representing major actors from global society. Three well-suited on-lookers with tall hats are the UK, CA (Canada) and Nato. They either fold their arms in front of their chests or hide their hands in their pockets, watching on while fire breaks out from the collision. China is portraited as fire-fighting, holding two fire extinguishers in its hands. Next to him, Uncle Sam points a finger at China and criticises: 'you are not doing your best!' while holding a fuel jug in the other hand, ready to add fuel to the fire. The article, correspondingly, criticises the US for escalating the crisis and praises China's efforts in peace making. These commentaries and cartoons over-simplify the complex reasons behind the war and mislead China's domestic readers' perception of action vs reaction as the real cause for Ukraine's resistance to invasion and Nato's aid to Ukraine.

Is China really neutral over Ukraine?

Although China's neutral position on Russia-Ukraine War seems to be consistent with its long-held foreign policy of non-interference in the domestic affairs of other countries, my analysis suggests that by implementing the three strategies of absence, framing and digression in reporting, Chinese media deliberately misrepresents the war and its resulting humanitarian crisis. Hanns W. Maull argues that China's neutrality is rooted in an interest-oriented 'maximin' strategy' that entails maximizing the economic benefits it can gain while minimizing the negative consequence of offending Russia (Maull, 2022). I would add that by denigrating the US for 'causing' the war, Chinese media also stokes up hatred towards the Western world aiding Ukraine's resistance to invasion. Elizabeth Wishnick (2017) observes that the China-Russia relationship is built upon 'the growing normative affinities' which present them jointly as an alternative force to the Western dominated global economy and value systems. China has resorted to public diplomacy instead of confrontations in solving global crises in the past decades (Wu, et al., 2021). However, its current position on the Ukraine War, as revealed by its official media, shows a tendency to pull away from Western engagement.

Now that the Ukraine War has entered its fourth month, the world is plagued with a gloomy prediction of prolonged humanitarian crisis, economic recession, food shortage, China-US tensions, and other risks. As the world's second largest economy, and one of the permanent members of UN Security Council, China's position has global implications. If China's 'neutral position' on Ukraine war means to prioritize its ties with Russia, it will only bring a deepened geopolitical division in the world and a possible negative long-term influence over future global crisis.

Note

[1] The Belt and Road Initiative (BRI) was first proposed by Chinese President Xi Jinpin in 2013, showing China's ambition to forge economic collaboration globally and build world new economic order centring around China's strategic development. Ever since 2013, China has invested more than half of trillion dollars in infrastructure, trade, finance and other sectors in countries signed up for the BRI programme.

References

CCTV, 2022. *Russian Military Tropes Entering Azovstal Steel Plant for Mine Clearance.* [Online]
Available at: https://photo.cctv.com/2022/05/24/
PHOA48xnoQzxDJS1dRbxW2LV220524.shtml?spm=C94212.PBi4fu284lJm.EqrnPf7
WDfbU.55#IBnr6ju7L0Uu220524_1
China Digital Times, 2022. *Minitrue: Four Leaked CAC Censorship Directives on Ukraine, Beijing Olympic Budget and Ban of Russian and Belarusian Paralympians.* [Online]
Available at: https://chinadigitaltimes.net/2022/03/minitrue-four-leaked-cac-censorship-directives-on-ukraine-beijing-olympic-budget-and-ban-of-russian-and-belarusian-paralympians/
China Digital Times, 2022. *Minitrue: Keep Weibo Posts on Ukraine Favorable to Russian; Control Comments.* [Online]
Available at: https://chinadigitaltimes.net/2022/02/minitrue-keep-weibo-posts-on-ukraine-favorable-to-russia-control-comments/
Gerasymchuk, S. & Poita, Y., 2018. *Ukraine-China after 2014: A new chapter in the relationship.* [Online]
Available at: https://library.fes.de/pdf-files/bueros/ukraine/14703.pdf
Maull, H. W., 2022. *Why China isn't backing away from alignment with Russia.* [Online]
Available at: https://thediplomat.com/2022/04/why-china-isnt-backing-away-from-alignment-with-russia/
Wang, J., 2022. *Xijian Wang.* [Online]

Available at: https://youtube.com/shorts/O3y_d-IM_S8?feature=share

Wishnick, E., 2017. In search of the 'other' in Asia: Russia-China relations revisited. *The Pacific Review*, 30(1), pp. 114-132.

Wu, Y., Thomas, R. & Yu, Y., 2021. From External Propaganda to Mediated Public Diplomacy: The Construction of the Chinese Dream in President Xi Jinping's New Year Speeches. In: *Public Diplomacy and the Politics of Uncertainty*. Cham: Palgrave Macmillan, pp. 29-55.

Xinhua, 2019. *China, Russia agree to upgrade relations for new era.* [Online]
Available at: http://www.china.org.cn/world/2019-06/06/content_74859445.htm

About the contributor

Dr Yan Wu is an Associate Professor in Media and Communication Studies, Swansea University. Her research interests focus on Chinese digital media and communication and digital inclusivity for sensory impaired users. Her publications appear in journals such as *New Media and Society*, *Global Media and China*, *International Journal of Digital Television*, *Modern Communication* and as book chapters in *Media and Public Sphere* (Palgrave Macmillan, 2007), *Climate Change and Mass Media* (Peter Lang, 2008), *Migration and the Media* (Peter Lang, 2012), *and Public Diplomacy and the Politics of Uncertainty* (Palgrave Macmillan, 2021).

China's poor reporting of the Ukraine War reveals our own failings

Marcus Ryder has been inside the belly of the Chinese media beasts - state and independent. He has seen the flaws and shortcomings but argues they are not peculiar to China

"Happy families are all alike; every unhappy family is unhappy in its own way. "

Anna Karenina - Leo Tolstoy

When discussing how journalism has covered the war in Ukraine it might be inappropriate to quote the famous Russian writer Leo Tolstoy. On the other hand it might be the best of times.

"Chinese journalism" is often seen as an oxymoron, however I believe studying how it has covered the war in Ukraine provides valuable lessons for journalists outside of China and our own journalistic practices.

First a little personal background

I have extensive experience, and inside knowledge, of Chinese media, as I worked for both its state media and "independent" media in China from 2016 - 2020. (Independent is in inverted commas not to signify that I believe there *isn't* independent media in China, but instead to acknowledge that independent media is heavily regulated and operates within confined parameters.)

I initially worked at CGTN (China Global Television Network) China's international facing state broadcaster, at what promised to be an exciting time and potential turning point in China's approach to international journalism. After two years I then moved to Caixin media in 2019 - China's equivalent of the *Financial Times*.

The dates are important.

In 2015 the British government's Digital Culture Media and Sport ministry signed a Memorandum of Understanding with the Chinese government over a range of issues. Change was in the air.

In 2016 the *Daily Mail* then started to carry paid content from the *People's Daily* (a prominent Chinese Communist Party newspaper) a practice copied by *the Daily Telegraph and the New York Times*. Simultaneously, in non-news content there was an active period of constructive engagement with China's state-sanctioned broadcasters and CGTN in particular. For instance, in 2016 Lion TV announced a deal with CGTN to co-produce "Chinese New Year: The Biggest Celebration on Earth" for the BBC.

Why did CCTV hire me?

I was brought in as China rebranded its state broadcaster *"CCTV English"* (China Central Television, English language) to "CGTN" to be more appealing to an international audience. As it tried to do so, there seemed a possibility that CGTN might effectively take what has become known as the *"Al Jazeera approach"*. In essence, it is one broadcaster with two different sets of news values: A domestic channel which seems to align itself with government positions regarding domestic policy (*Al Jazeera*) and an international facing broadcasting channel which can exercise independent journalism relatively free from political interference and with more internationally recognised journalistic standards (*Al Jazeera English*).

I recognise that numerous PhDs have been written about *Al Jazeera* and *Al Jazeera English*, and I am making massive generalisations, but for the sake of brevity I believe this is the best way to understand the general principles of what was occurring in China around 2016.

As a former BBC news executive, my job was largely "capacity building" - training young and older journalists from literally all around the world to cover stories in an objective and balanced manner, and try to instil news values into journalists from China and other countries where some of these elements have been, at best, dormant and, at worst, suppressed.

The dream falls apart

The hope - possibly naively - that it would become the *Al Jazeera English* of Chinese state broadcasting began to fade in 2019 when international scrutiny on the democracy protests in Hong Kong and the treatment of Uighurs in the west of China increased significantly, and the Chinese government - and CGTN - more or less retrenched to old practices.

It was at this point that I left CGTN and moved to *Caixin*. A news organisation frequently cited by China experts as one of the best, if not the best, news organisations of "independent" journalism in China.

In particular, I was fortunate enough to be still working at *Caixin* during the outbreak of the Covid-19 pandemic and I would argue its fearless reporting in Wuhan - the original epicentre of the virus - literally saved millions of lives globally, informing both domestic and international policy responses to the pandemic.

Chinese broadcasting from the inside

I share all this as a prelude to explain how and why, in many ways, my work in China was the most rewarding and at the same time frustrating time I have ever experienced as a journalist. However, importantly, it gave me a unique insight into how China's state broadcasting and independent media operated.

It also means I often bristle when Chinese journalism is often simply dismissed as "just propaganda", and its journalists as being lackeys of the state.

The reality is Chinese journalism is multifaceted and on an individual basis, many of the Chinese journalists I met were just as principled - for better and for worse - as most journalists I work with in the UK.

So, let us return to that famous Tolstoy quote; "Happy families are all alike; every unhappy family is unhappy in its own way."

Similarly, good journalism is all alike: high journalistic standards, speaking truth to power without fear or favour, containing all relevant facts necessary to fully inform an audience to understand the issues.

Bad journalism in China

Indeed, every example of bad journalism is bad in its own way. China's record of bad journalism is well documented.

In 2021, China's "press freedom index", as measured by Reporters Without Borders (RSF), was 78.72 points, placing the fourth lowest in 180 surveyed countries in the world, just above the totalitarian countries of Turkmenistan, North Korea and Eritrea.

However, it is in exploring the challenges facing journalists trying to produce good journalism - in a range of situations - that we as journalists learn the most about ourselves.

And that is why China's coverage of Ukraine is so important.

Analysing China's media coverage of the war forces us to go back to journalistic first principles and even forces those of us outside of China to reflect on the quality of the journalism from outside of China, including from the UK, when it comes to the war.

Is Chinese journalism 'impartial'?

For instance, when we journalists outside of China criticise Chinese journalism for not being impartial - we should dissect why we think it fails the partiality test - and in so doing set up the criteria that *all* journalistic impartiality should be judged by.

Or, when we criticise Chinese journalism for being a "mouthpiece of the government" - we should use that as a tool by which to judge how much our own journalism reflects the values of our own governments, and how much we really "speak truth to power".

It is not useful to look at Chinese media and crow over how much better our journalism is.

We already know that.

However, it is useful to look at how the Chinese "journalistic family is unhappy" and use that to see how we can improve our own journalism.

And so, let us explore the two examples above in more detail.

The first thing the war forces journalists to confront is the principle of "impartiality".

What might be surprising to many is Chinese media views itself as impartial when it comes to coverage of the war and Western media as biased. This is not just a propaganda line asserted by the Chinese government, but is a genuinely held belief by several foreign and Chinese journalists working for Chinese media to whom I have spoken.

In February 2022 China abstained from a UN Security Council vote condemning the invasion of Ukraine. As the BBC's China correspondent Stephen McDonell wrote, "Some analysts had expected Beijing to join Russia in voting against the motion, but the fact that it did not has been described as a "win for the West" - and is a sign of Beijing's non-interference."

The principle of "non-interference" is central to China's foreign policy stance and can be traced back to the Bandung (Non-Aligned) conference of 1955.

Several other countries most notably; India, South Africa and Pakistan - along with numerous other African, Asian and South American countries - also either abstained or were deliberately not present at the time of the vote.

An 'overwhelming' UN vote against Russia?

The vote however was presented in Western media as a demonstration that the world condemned Russia's actions with many pointing to the fact that 141 of the 193 member states voted for the resolution, with many publications including *Reuters*, the *Guardian,* and the *Wall Street Journal,* amongst others, using the word "overwhelmingly".

In CGTN, reporting of the vote was far more "flat" with the headline: "The UN General Assembly adopts a draft resolution on Ukraine".

As a former news editor, I would argue that the CGTN headline does not properly reflect the gravity and importance of the UN vote. However, it also forces me to question whether Western media covered it correctly in using words such as "overwhelmingly" when thinking of the vote not in terms of country numbers but population size and/or regional economic importance.

The second major issue is whether Chinese state media is a "mouthpiece" for the Chinese government. The short answer of course is, "yes".

Are the 'independent' media in China still just that?

However, looking at China's "independent" media, such as *Caixin,* illustrates that there is a spectrum of views on Ukraine within China. As early as March 7 2022, Caixin was describing the Russian invasion as a "war", despite the Chinese government and state media opting to use the Russian euphemism "special military operation".

Caixin has also been quite clear that Russia is the aggressor in the war.

Caixin, although not state media, is one of the most important media outlets in China.

This spectrum of views on the war from CGTN to *Caixin* should motivate us, as thorough, curious and intellectually rigorous journalists outside of China and including in the UK, to pause and reflect on the range of "acceptable" views on the war. It should motivate us to examine - for instance when BBC journalist, Clive Myrie, tweets that "http://S.Africa's Ramaphosa blames Nato for Russia's war in Ukraine https://reuters.com/world/africa/sa- Utter crap!!!" - whether we are giving a fair hearing to views we might not agree..

These are just two examples of journalistic principles that looking at Chinese media enable us to explore but many others exist:

Embedded with the enemy?

Chinese journalists have been criticised for being embedded with the Russian army, with the suggestion that this proves their lack of "impartiality". But what does this say about the conditions that our journalists should accept when embedded with *any* military force? Is this a practice that requires more debate?

Chinese state media for a domestic audience has been criticised for not giving Ukraine enough prominence. But what does that say about the copious amounts of coverage we have dedicated to the war at the possible expense of other conflicts around the world?

This is not whataboutism

The flaws in Chinese journalism are well documented.

But my time working in China forced me to examine issues in journalistic practices I took for granted in the UK. As a journalist, I believe looking at Chinese media should also be a reflective exercise about our own coverage of the Ukraine war.

Pointing fingers at the flaws in Chinese coverage at best tells us what we already know and at worst stops us looking at the flaws in our own journalism.

To build on Tolstoy's quote and at the risk of destroying one of the greatest lines in literature: We shouldn't just look at the unhappiness of other families. Even if we are happier, we should also look at our own unhappiness, and strive to avoid it.

About the contributor

Marcus Ryder MBE is the co-founder of the Sir Lenny Henry Centre for Media Diversity. A former executive producer of BBC Scotland Current Affairs programmes and multiple award-winning journalist he has written extensively on the issues of foreign reporters seeing the world through a "white male gaze".

Afterword

Why the war in Ukraine matters

What is happening in Ukraine, and how it is reported, should constitute a belated wake-up call to the West, argues Sky News' Security and Defence Editor, Deborah Haynes. Travelling with UK Defence Secretary Ben Wallace in Oslo on 14 June 2022 she filed this exclusive for this book

The carnage in Ukraine is horrific, yet as Russia's invasion drags on it is already starting to slip down the news agenda in the UK and across the western world. But ignore the biggest war in Europe since 1945 at your peril.

Moscow's missiles, of course, pose the acutest threat to Ukraine. But the actions of Vladimir Putin have exposed the limitations of western power in a world where authoritarian states like Russia and more importantly China are on the rise. If left unchecked, events in Ukraine could still mark a fundamental shift in the balance of global power. This is true even if the invasion fails to produce a decisive victory for either side and instead freezes in a bloody stalemate with Ukrainian land still held by Russia.

Make no mistake, Putin and his generals are responsible for unleashing hell on their neighbour. But Russia's decision even to attempt a full-scale assault on Ukraine was also a product of decades of complacency, miscalculation, and botched diplomacy by western allies.

Their flawed statecraft was further exacerbated by a failure of British and other European governments to understand and then relay in a convincing way to their respective publics the importance of security and in investing in a credible military.

It is a dereliction of duty that endured in the face of repeated signals that Moscow was an increasingly hostile state – and always had been despite the end of the Cold War.

Warning signs

Consider the Salisbury spy poisonings in 2018; the meddling in the US presidential election in 2016; or a crippling cyber-attack against the Baltic state of Estonia in 2007. Those actions, attributed to Russia, took place in a grey zone of harm that sits deliberately under the threshold of war. It is a place where everything can be – and is – used as a weapon, from cyber hacks and social media posts to politics

139

and energy. Such covert warfare is designed to be deniable, making it harder to call out and deter than a more conventional armed attack. That said, even violating a nation's sovereignty can be masked in the grey zone as Moscow demonstrated with its first invasion of Ukraine back in 2014.

Over the years, each time Russia - and similarly China - dared to test the West's resolve by violating global rules, rights and values, the UK and its allies failed to impose a high enough cost to deter future hostilities. A misguided peacetime mentality and a self-serving desire for Russian and Chinese investment influenced policy and meant punches were too often pulled.

This slowly eroded the existing international order, grown from the ashes of the Second World War and designed to help democracies flourish and authoritarian regimes flounder.

Add into the mix a so-called "peace dividend" that British and other European governments have sought to enjoy since the collapse of the Soviet Union. It led to public spending over the past 30 years being diverted from costly defence projects into more popular, vote-winning sectors like health, education, and the economy.

Nato's gamble

The size and capability - and as a result ability to deter and defend - of many militaries within the Nato alliance then shrank. The UK's reduction was particularly stark given its historic strength and status as a military power.

By contrast, Moscow continued to invest heavily in its armed forces and malign activities.

Even as realisation gradually dawned that Russia was not a friend, there was no corresponding switchback to a wartime posture. Instead, for most western governments, it was a case of focus on whatever immediate crisis is splashed on the front pages and hope to avoid being caught out by the ever greater risk being taken with defence and security.

This was not a secret. Military and security officials who understood the threat repeatedly raised the alarm – most noisily once they had retired. But to no avail. They started to predict the West's complacency would only be reversed by a strategic shock that would expose the hollowing out of their defences, hopefully before the rot became irreversible.

That shock came on 24 February 2022 – the day western deterrence comprehensively failed. Two events stand out in the run-up to Russia's invasion. First was a joint statement by Putin and China's Xi Jinping that set out their shared vision of what they called a "new era" in international relations. Unveiled in Beijing at the start of the Winter Olympics and as more than 120,000 Russian troops massed at Ukraine's borders, it offered a deliberately public show of unity – even though analysts say the two authoritarian regimes lack any true sense of mutual trust.

The second event came a fortnight later, when western leaders met at an annual security conference in the German city of Munich. Warnings from US, British and other delegates about an imminent Russian invasion of Ukraine dominated. The allies were united in their calls for Putin to pull back.

Kamala Harris, the US Vice President, told the Munich Security Conference: "If Russia further invades Ukraine, the United States, together with our allies and partners, will impose significant and unprecedented economic costs [...] And we will not stop with economic measures. We will further reinforce our Nato allies on the eastern flank."

The unthinkable happens

From my vantage point in the Ukrainian capital Kyiv at the time, the sense of the West talking to itself within its own echo chamber never felt so great or the words so vacuous.

Less than a week later, Russia's war began. What most European leaders had considered to be the unthinkable was the new reality. A planned lighting strike on Kyiv was only averted because the prowess of Russia's war machine turned out to be as phony as the excuse Putin gave to deploy it.

The strength of Ukraine's resistance was also a significant factor. But that was not known by the allies in those first few days. It was only at the darkest of points, with the first Russian missiles hitting Ukrainian cities and tanks rolling onto Ukrainian roads, that the West appeared finally to wake up to the existential threat Putin's nuclear-armed Russia posed not just to Ukraine but to all of Europe.

For once, the European Union was united in revulsion against Moscow and resolved to fight back - as was Nato. Incredibly, Finland and Sweden, two historically neutral states, decided they wanted to join the alliance. A western officer said allies joked about Putin being Nato's employee of the year. "He's done more to galvanise the alliance in three months that anyone else!" the officer told me.

Even Germany, the economic powerhouse of Europe but with a weak military, made stunning new pledges to increase its own paltry - in relative terms - defence spending, wean itself off Russian gas and oil, and send weapons to Ukraine.

But will this new resolve endure as the fickle nature of many western governments with an inability to think beyond an election cycle kicks in? Russia will also be seeking in the grey zone to exploit divisions within the EU and Nato. It is already using its stronghold on energy supplies to inflict pain and leverage influence.

Ben Wallace, the UK defence secretary, has been a leading voice, pushing allies to do more to arm and equip Ukraine, while also bolster Nato's defences. He said there is a "real challenge to the global world order, to our values, by a number of countries, including China, including Russia".

This was something allies had already faced during the Cold War. "It isn't new, we just have to be reminded that there is no free lunch. You can't stand up for your values without spending and investing in your capabilities to do so," he told me in an interview for this book.

As for whether he believed allies have the conviction to turn big pledges to respond to the Russian threat into meaningful action, Mr Wallace said: "They have actually put money where their mouth is." But he added: "I think there are one or two countries in Europe where they think that somehow... it [Ukraine] is a country a long way away of which we know nothing and can't we all get back to our sun loungers?"

The West's failure

Unfortunately, the West's track record on staying the course in a crisis in recent years is dismal. But Russia's war has delivered the biggest challenge to European security since Adolf Hitler. This has created an opportunity by jolting decision-makers into understanding the need to make their militaries fit for 21st century warfare. If that realisation is acted upon, there is a hope that what US President Joe Biden, prior to the Ukraine crisis, "an inflection point in world history" – the pitting of democracy once more against the rise of authoritarianism – will see a sustained push back against Russia and China.

However, if this eleventh hour opportunity to react is squandered as the war in Ukraine slips off the front pages and the attention of western governments is distracted by more immediate and less complicated crises then the future is bleak, and not only for Ukraine.

History could well look back on Russia's invasion as the moment the international rules drawn up in the wake of World War II unravelled and a new global order, this time favouring authoritarian rule, was born.

About the contributor

Deborah Haynes has worked for TV Tokyo, Agence France-Presse, Reuters, and *The Times* where she was Defence Editor. Since September 2018 she has been Foreign Affairs Editor and then Security and Defence Editor for *Sky News*. She won the inaugural Bevins Prize, as well as an Amnesty International UK Media Award for her reporting on the dangers faced by Iraqi interpreters after British troops withdrew from the country.

Lightning Source UK Ltd.
Milton Keynes UK
UKHW020717220722
406233UK00006B/681